The Royal Hundred of Cookham

Written by Luke Over

Illustrated by Chris Tyrrell

This book is dedicated to John Brooks, a Cookham historian, who passed away in 1993.

Published & Printed by Cliveden Press
Priors Way, Bray, Maidenhead, Berkshire SL6 2HP
Tel: Maidenhead (0628) 75151 Fax: (0628) 773090

1994

Copyright © Text Luke Over, 1994
Copyright © Illustrations Chris Tyrrell, 1994

ISBN 0 9521969 1 3

Preface

This book is intended as a companion volume to *The Royal Hundred of Bray* produced by the same authors in 1993. The two volumes together cover the twin royal manors from which the town of Maidenhead evolved in the thirteenth century, and the smaller settlements which go to form its outer suburban area. The origins of all settlements are recorded.

The Royal Hundred of Cookham is dedicated to the memory of John Brooks (1921–93), who did so much to keep alive the history of the village. In 1976 he produced a short guide to Holy Trinity Church and its environs, which was illustrated with his own drawings and plans, some of which are reproduced in this book. In the following year he wrote a further volume for the Queen's Silver Jubilee. John was a modest and meticulous worker, and spent years transcribing documents and registers for the use of social historians and genealogists. The Brooks Marriage Index is internationally well known.

Cookham's earliest historian of note was the antiquarian Stephen Darby, who was born in the village in 1825. A qualified chemist, he worked for many years in the Cookham brewery owned by his father, Abraham Darby. After many years of comprehensive study he published the volume *Place and Field Names of Cookham Parish* (1899) which was followed by his master work *Chapters in the History of Cookham* in 1909. He died in his home at Starlings, Cookham Dean in December 1911. The proceeds from his book were donated to the Maidenhead Cottage Hospital.

The other major historical work on the village and its environs is *The Story of Cookham* (1990) by Robin and Valerie Bootle. Valerie works for the *Maidenhead Advertiser* and Robin writes and produces science and history programmes for television. This chatty and detailed book was produced to raise money for the church restoration fund.

The Royal Hundred of Cookham was not written with the intention of duplicating these earlier books, although by necessity many facts have been repeated. The present work however, covers a wider area as encompassed by the Hundred, which includes a part of Windsor Forest. In compiling the book the authors have combined evidence from primary and secondary sources, ancient documents, excavation, fieldwork and placenames.

The book is lavishly illustrated with high quality line drawings of buildings and scenes in the locality, together with some interesting documents and a selection of maps. In the production of this book the authors would like to thank Peter Morris of Cliveden Press for his continued faith in its success, Veronica Kempton for the typescript, and the Reverend David Rossdale, Vicar of Cookham, for writing the Foreword, which is particularly relevant as 1994 is the centenary year of the Parish Council, and the 150th anniversary of the building of St. John the Baptist Church, Cookham Dean.

Foreword

Stephen Darby, in his "Chapters in the History of Cookham" reflects that "Cookham as I remember it in the year of grace 1831 impressed one with its appearance of peacefulness and quietude". Those of us who live here in the closing decade of the twentieth century experience a very different village, with the rush and bustle of modern life. Yet just beneath the surface, we know that we live in a place steeped in history, which gives us a thirst to understand more.

Luke Over's authoritative and engaging work, brought to life by Chris Tyrell's illustrations, helps us to quench this thirst. As we move through the book, we discover ever more about the history of our fascinating village and its surroundings, reinforcing our awareness that we enjoy a rich heritage. This is a work to which we will frequently wish to return.

The Reverend David Rossdale,
Vicar of Cookham

Cookham Church in Winter

About the Authors

The writer, Luke Over, is acknowledged as a local historian and is well known for his lectures and the 200 articles he has written for the *Maidenhead Advertiser*. After studying archaeology at London University he spent 30 years excavating sites in the area and elsewhere including the Domesday site of Maidenhead. In the past 15 years he has concentrated on the history of the area, carrying out fieldwork, studying placenames and examining old documents, in the hope of discovering new facts about the early history of east Berkshire.

His literary achievements in this field include numerous articles for journals, local and national magazines and some 44 publications. His books *The Story of Maidenhead, Maidenhead – A Pictorial History* and *Domesday Revisited* proved to be popular best sellers on the local market, whilst *Furze Platt Remembered*, which he ghost wrote for Ray Knibbs, sold out in ten days.

Recently he has been talking about local history in a series of programmes on BBC Radio Berkshire and Cable Television. He is Secretary of the Berkshire Archaeological Society and a Vice President of the Maidenhead Archaeological & Historical Society, as well as serving on numerous other committees. His ambition is to promote an interest in local history and an understanding of the local environment.

The illustrator, Chris Tyrrell, was born at Hayes in Middlesex and studied art at the Twickenham College of Technology. After his initial training and during the 1960s he was guided in his work by the royal portrait painter Pietro Annigoni. During his career he has travelled extensively in Europe and the Far East producing paintings and sketches in Thailand, Hong Kong and China.

His paintings have been exhibited at the Royal Society of Portrait Painters, the Royal Society of British Artists, the Royal Society of Painter-Etchers and Engravers, the United Society of Artists and the Royal Institute Summer Salon. He is an elected member of the Society of Architectural Illustrators.

His one-man exhibition 'Around Maidenhead' in 1988 was opened by Her Grace the Duchess of Norfolk, on which occasion he presented a painting of Pine Lodge to the Thames Valley Hospice.

Much of his local work has been published as Christmas cards, calendars, postcards and in magazines. His paintings of Cookham were used in the book *The Story of Cookham*. Many of his paintings are in collections worldwide and various notable personalities collect his work. At present he is concentrating on landscapes and architectural subjects in watercolours.

Both authors combined their talents to produce *The Royal Hundred of Bray* during 1993, which is a companion volume to this book.

Contents

The Berkshire Hundreds (Emanuel Bowen c1758)

CHAPTER 1
Introducing Cookham Hundred

Today Cookham is a well sought after, picturesque village on the river Thames which attracts many tourists during the course of a year. Many arrive by boat in the summer and moor overnight, whilst others park the car and take a pleasant walk along the riverbank to Cockmarsh. Others drive to the summit of Winter Hill to enjoy the view over the Thames towards Marlow or explore the countryside lanes where many relics of its chequered past can be found.

The village is perhaps best known as the home of the artist Stanley Spencer, and many of his works can be seen in the Stanley Spencer Gallery in the High Street. It is also the home of the Turk family who for most of this century held the position of the royal Swanmaster and officiated at the annual swan-upping ceremony.

The division of land into territorial units as we see them today began in the Anglo-Saxon era. These took the form of administrative areas under either ecclesiastical or civil control. The unit of ecclesiastical control was the parish, the earliest of which was created in the sixth century with the coming of St Augustus to Britain. The first parishes normally covered a wide area, depending on the number of churches available for worship. The earliest type of parish church was the minster, which was usually a royal or episcopal foundation, under the control of a number of priests. As more churches became available from endowments provided by the upper classes, additional parishes were created making administration more manageable. In the early stages these were under the control of a rector rather than a vicar.

Before the eighth century AD, Britain was divided into *provinciae*, the earliest known units of local government which originated in Roman times. By the year 800, Wessex at least had been divided up into *hundreds*, which were notionally an area of 100 hides of land, or 12,000 acres, but in practice were not usually that precise. Within the hundreds were a series of *manors*, smaller self-sufficient agricultural units, which in most cases have developed into modern villages. Each manor was controlled by a tenant-in-chief who held a manor house, and consisted of arable, meadow and woodland and were situated near water, mills and fisheries. When manors coincided with parishes there was also a parish church.

In the context of these early boundaries, the parish of Cookham was probably formed in the seventh century as Christianity was introduced in Wessex and the Thames Valley in AD 634 by Birinus, a bishop from Rome, who created a *see* at Dorchester-on-Thames. The existence of a pre-Conquest church at Cookham cannot be confirmed with certainty, the

The Seven Hundreds of Cookham and Bray (Robert Morden c1695)

first mention of a building being in the Domesday Survey c. 1086. However, evidence suggests that Cookham may have been a minster because of its royal foundation. The existence of a monastery in Cookham by the year 700 would have by necessity ensured the existence of an early church, albeit that it was only for the use of the monks and nuns.

The lands with which the Cookham monastery was endowed were considerable and may have spread across the whole of East Berkshire. Before this date the same area was part of the provincia of *Suninges* and came under the Bishopric of Salisbury. This vast ecclesiastical estate spread from the present village of Sonning for some distance to the east and eastwards as far as Sunninghill, which derives its name from the same source.

The first mention of Berkshire as a county was in AD 860 when it was recorded as *Berrocscir* and took its name from a wood near Hungerford. The earliest details of the county are given in the Domesday Survey c. 1086 where it is shown that the shire was subdivided into 22 hundreds which in turn were broken up into 192 manors. In this survey Cookham was situated in the Hundred of Beynhurst, which stretched from the Thames to the Surrey border, and also included Bisham, Hurley, Elentone, White Waltham, Shottesbrooke and Waltham St Lawrence.

For two hundred years from Domesday numerous boundary changes took place within the hundreds and many were given new names. The Hundred of Cookham had been formed in its own right by 1250 and it is mentioned in 1268 when Roger de Fryht is returned as 'bailiff of the Seven Hundreds of Beynhurst, Ripplesmere, Charlton, Bray, Cookham, Sonning and Wargrave'. In 1225 a perambulation of East Berkshire by the Windsor Forest Justices had led to the formation of the Liberty of the Forest, later known as the Liberty of the Seven Hundreds and then by 1296 as the Seven Hundreds of Cookham and Bray. The court associated with this was the chief court for the forest district, and the idea was to ensure uniform administration in the King's hunting area and to inflict severe penalties on anyone interfering with the royal game.

The Hundred of Cookham as defined and described in this book includes Cookham Village, Cookham Rise, Cookham Dean, Pinkneys Green, Furze Platt, Stubbings and

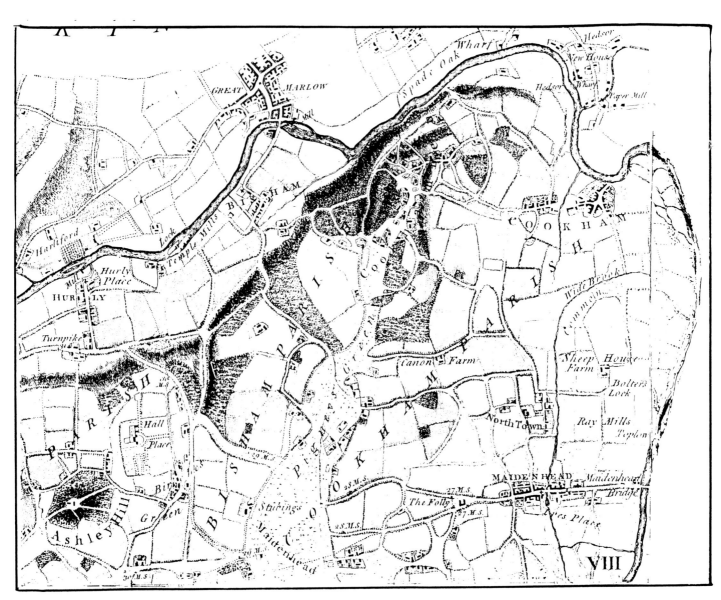

Cookham in 1761 (John Rocque)

14

North Town, all settlements that have come into existence at different times. The boundary to the south was the Bath Road stretching from the Shire Horse on Maidenhead Thicket to the Bridge passing through the centre of Maidenhead High Street. Other areas now absorbed into Maidenhead are parts of the parishes of St Mary's and St Lukes and the Ray Estate bordering on the river. In addition to these the settlements of Binfield and Sunninghill, originally in the Forest of Windsor, are included. During the seventeenth century the inhabitants of Sunninghill were described as 'mean men, their grounds barren, and the deer seldom out of them', whereas Cookham and Binfield were occupied by men of great estate.

Royal interest in the hundred and manor of Cookham is due to its proximity to the palace and castle at Windsor. The Domesday Book mentions the palace of the Saxon kings at Old Windsor and the 95 *hagae* or house plots that surrounded the palace complex and were in use as residences for the officials of the court. The castle at New Windsor was built in 1070 in the manor of Clewer for the defence of the realm, but succeeded the old palace as a royal residence when Henry I took over the building in the year 1110. Cookham became Crown property from AD 975 when the will of Aelpheah, the head man of the shire, records that 'he gives his royal lord the land at Cookham'. The king in question was Edgar (959–975), who died soon afterwards. Nevertheless, Cookham remained with the Crown until 1818, and with the exception of the period 1399–1447 when it was held by Humphrey, Duke of Gloucester, it was part of the dowry of the Queens of England from 1303 to 1547.

The name Cookham is not very imaginative, and has puzzled etymologists over the years. Variations include *Coccham (798), Cocham (997), Cocheham (1086), Cokeham (1265), Cokham (1327)* and *Cookham (1399)*. The elements are Anglo-Saxon, the suffix *ham* meaning settlement and the prefix *cocc* indicating a hillock, a cock bird, or a cook. The prefix *Coch*, as in the earlier versions of the name can also be read as *Cox* as featured in the placename Coxburrow at Cookham rise. Most agree that Cookham means 'Cook Village', but refers to a trade rather than a personal name, although who the cook was nobody knows.

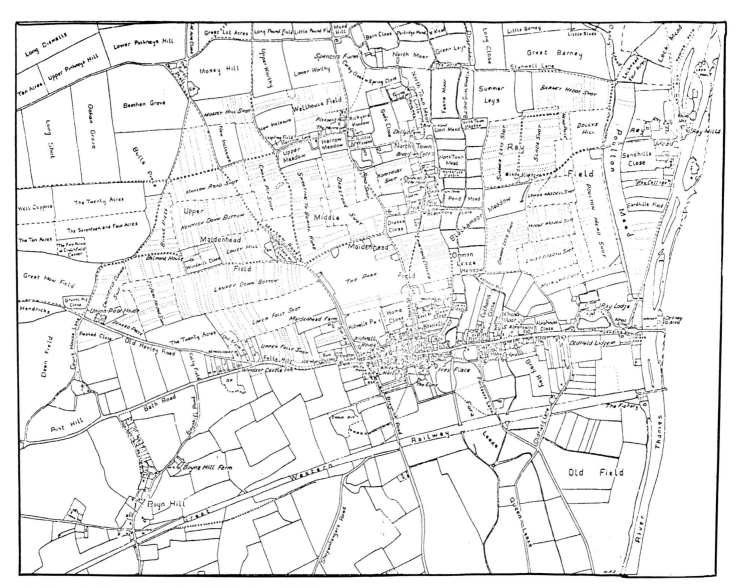

Cookham field names north of Maidenhead 1840

CHAPTER 2
Cookham Genesis

The landscape of Cookham Hundred, with the exception of the outlying settlements of Binfield and Sunninghill, form part of the Thames Valley which was fashioned during a series of Ice Ages, which occurred during the last half a million years of geological time. The settlement is situated at one end of the Chilterns, whose solid geology is chalk and flint laid down as crushed seashells and marine organisms below the cretaceous seas some 200 million years ago.

In the last 500,000 years there have been three glaciations during which the ice built up and moved forwards changing the landscape in its wake. During the intervening interglacial periods, the ice retreated and melted, producing fast flowing torrents which carved through the chalk to a depth of 150 feet leaving a valley through which the Thames flowed. Throughout this process the river formed flood plains at varying heights, and gravel terraces which are named after places in the Maidenhead area because of early studies carried out there.

The highest Thames terraces are the oldest and occur as Winter Hill (150 feet), Boyn Hill (100 feet), Lynch Hill or Furze Platt (65 feet), Taplow (40 feet) and the present flood plain. It was on these terraces that the nomadic hunter-gatherers of the Old Stone Age or *Palaeolithic* period first created their flimsy shelters of wood and animal hide, and fashioned stone tools and hand axes from the abundant supplies of flint in the area.

As can be seen from the published map the present flood plain, which stretches from Cookham to Bray, is very extensive and as such has influenced the course of history in

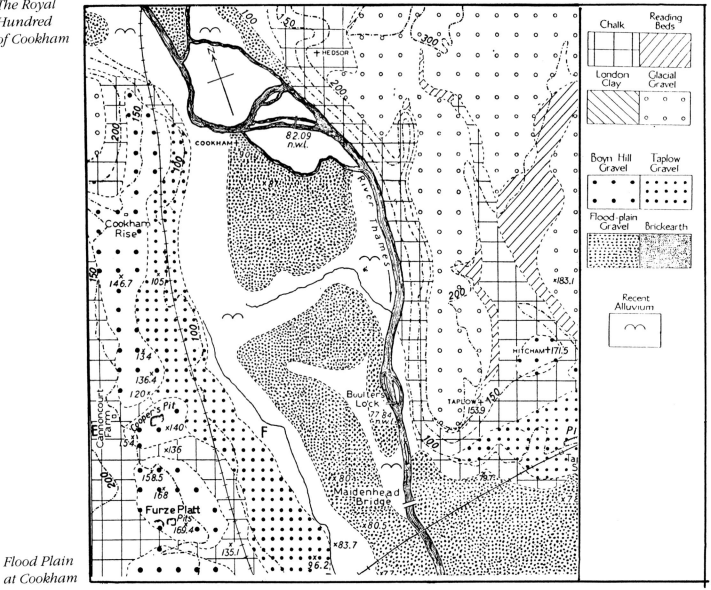

the area. Above the flood plain are the Taplow and Boyn Hill terraces which have been subject to gravel extraction over the past one hundred years. During these excavations large quantities of flint hand axes came to light in Hamfield, Cookham Rise and Kinghorn Pit in Cannon Court Road, Furze Platt, shown on the map as Coopers Pit. This latter site is one of the most prolific in Britain and has yielded over 2,000 *Palaeolithic* hand axes, a large proportion of which are in the British Museum. We can only guess at the lifestyle of these early nomads, as their stone implements are all that survive.

The Old Stone Age, which is subject to numerous sub-divisions, was a long period, lasting from at least 350,000 down to 10,000 BC, when the present flood plain of the Thames was established. At this time *Mesolithic*, or Middle Stone Age man appears to have migrated from the Continent and settled on the smaller streams and tributaries of the Thames. Their main tool was the Thames pick, which was supplemented by an assemblage of *microliths*, or minute flint tools, which when hafted were suitable for the spearing of fish.

Palaeolithic Handaxes

Excavation at numerous sites on the Thames flood plain has revealed that Stone Age Man regularly settled there, perhaps during a period when the river was at its lowest level. However, evidence of occupation during the *Mesolithic* or the succeeding *Neolithic* period seems to be scanty in the Cookham area and confined to a few casual finds of pottery and flints. The *Neolithic*, or New Stone Age, period, which began around 4,000 BC, heralded the first farmers in Britain who were looking for arable land on which to cultivate their crops of wheat, emmer and spelt, early cereals previously developed in the Middle East. One of their major innovations was the introduction of crude pottery, which replaced the animal hide as a container for the storage of food and water.

The nearest site of this period is located at Bray, but evidence of their existence comes from polished hand axes that have been dredged from the Thames. A boat that can probably be attributed to this period was raised from the bed of the Thames near the

Bourne End bank in 1871. The vessel was 25 feet long by 3 foot wide and was found in 16 foot of water buried in a bed of sand. It had been carved from a solid oak tree with a pointed bow and a square stern. There were two seats at the stern which had been formed from solid wood. When found it was put on display at the Fisheries Museum in South Kensington, but like so many Victorian finds has been lost or destroyed since that time.

The long usage of stone for making effective but rather cumbersome tools came to an end in 1800 BC when bronze smiths from the Mediterranean brought to Britain the knowledge of metal working. The tools of the *Bronze Age*, made from an alloy of tin and copper, were sophisticated for their time and the old stone hand axe was superseded by socketed metal axeheads, which when hafted were much easier to use. Examples of bronze implements have also been dredged from the river.

On Cockmarsh Common there are four *tumuli* which date to this period, of which only one is immediately visible. These were barrows or burial mounds, some 90 foot across and 8 foot in height, in which important people were interred. Bronze Age burial mounds are not common in East Berkshire, and it is unusual to find them located on low ground as at Cookham. This group of four were investigated in 1874 by local antiquarians Cocks and Napier, and two of them were found to contain the remains of cremated bodies. The largest of the *tumuli* contained a portion of a jawbone which enabled the experts to identify the remains as that of a female. The burial was accompanied by the skull of an ox, thought to be the remains of a funeral feast. The other mound contained the remains of a child. We obviously do not know the identity of the deceased, but such elaborate burials suggest they may have been the wife and child of a local chieftain.

Excavation in Switchback Road, above Lower Mount Farm, in recent years has produced some activity of the *Bronze Age* peoples, otherwise evidence is limited to occasional finds in the area. One group of cropmarks as seen from the air in a field adjacent to Widbrook Common suggest that a farmstead of this period may lie beneath the ground.

The Cockmarsh Tumulus

Evidence of early *Iron Age* occupation after these new metal workers appeared on the scene around 500 BC, occurs at Mount Hill, Cookham Dean where a small enclosure of this period crowns the hill. The earthwork is situated in a position whereby its occupiers could overlook a vast stretch of country and as such was probably defensive. The large hillforts of the *Iron Age* are well known, though none exist in Cookham, the nearest examples being at Medmenham and High Wycombe.

Excavation at Mount Hill carried out by local antiquarian Stephen Darby in 1907 revealed two hut circles and a number of fragments of coarse pottery of the period as was similarly found at the nearby Pigeonhouse Wood. Other artifacts, including a spindle whorl were also located. Evidence of farmsteads of this period, which invariably occur on lower ground, appears to be lacking.

By 100 BC the last of the prehistoric settlers had reached Southern Britain. These were the *Belgae*, a tribe from the continent, who had had experience of Roman occupation. These were an advanced people, who brought with them the knowledge of wheel-made pottery, the first coinage and a plan for the first towns in Britain. These were known as *oppida* and comprised a settlement surrounded by a defensive ditch or *vallum*, and were usually situated in the low lying areas. The majority of these Belgic towns were taken over and used by the Romans after their invasion in AD 43. The town that governed the area of Cookham was the *oppidum* at Calleva, south of Reading, which was the capital of the *Atrebates* tribe, and the site of a Belgic mint.

Similarly, small Belgic farmsteads were taken over by the Romans and turned into villa-farms, as will be discussed later. One such settlement was discovered during gravel digging in 1958 close by the railway line at SU 885838. The site showed an occupation from 1st to the 4th centuries AD, of which the earliest phase was represented by a rectangular enclosure, made up in its remaining parts by a series of shallow V-shaped ditches. Post holes found inside the enclosure and at its entrance may well have outlined a hut and a gatehouse. There was a large quantity of Belgic pottery, but all other finds dated to the Roman period, showing a re-use of the site.

Ten years later, in 1968, further excavations took place nearby at SU 885841 by the mobile home park at Strande Castle. Here again Belgic pottery was found stratified at the lowest levels of a boundary ditch, which was later used by the Romans.

The other main site of this period in the Hundred of Cookham is the better known Robin Hood's Arbour, on Maidenhead Thicket near Stubbings. Naturally it has no connection with the Prince of Thieves from Sherwood Forest, nor is it a Roman Camp as suggested on many early maps. The history of this site is interesting and probably deserves some space.

Robin Hood's Arbour is a ditched rectilinear enclosure of about three quarters of an acre. Its form is sub-rectangular, its sides measuring: North 144 feet; East 210 feet; South 230 feet; West 156 feet. The enclosing ditch has an inner bank built with spoil from the ditch and in places there is a counterscarp bank. The ditch is missing on the west side for 65 feet north of the entrance.

The earliest reference traced was that of Kerry in 1861, who favoured a Roman origin for the earthwork and wrote, "As an argument in favour of its antiquity, it should be remembered that the thicket has never been cultivated, and that until comparatively modern times there were but few habitations in the locality; any remains, therefore, existing thereon, corresponding as they do with the known habits and systems of a primitive people, must of necessity be a work of the former, and not the productions of a later age".

Bannard, in his article on Maidenhead Thicket in 1931, tells us that in 1894 "Mr Rutland and Mr Henry Arrowsmith made an exhaustive investigation of Robin Hood's

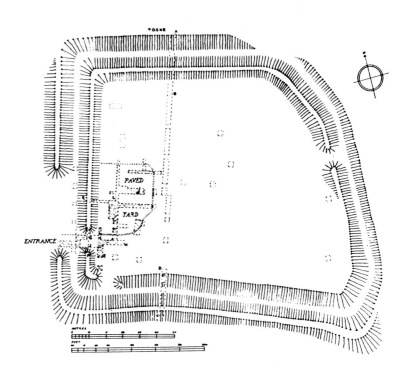

Robin Hood's Arbour

Arbour by digging there, but the results were very disappointing, very few remains of any interest and none of any great importance being found".

In 1950, Mrs M A Cotton directed an excavation on the site on behalf of the Berkshire Field Research Group and, as a result of this, we have a clearer picture of the purpose of the earthwork.

The defences were sectioned on the north and south sides and partially on the western. The sections were similar and the north side will serve as a good example. The ditch here was found to be 16 feet wide and 2 feet 9 inches deep, U-shaped and cut through clay loam and clay just short of solid chalk. The loam from the ditch was used to make the inner bank, and flints used to consolidate the banks were found to be in "mint" condition and not derived from the spot but brought in from elsewhere. There were no indications of a palisade, or of timbering being used in the defences. The only 'finds' from the defences occurred on the north side and comprised a hand-made cooking pot from the bank, a wheel-turned sherd from primary silt in the ditch and a metacarpal of an ox or cow from the bank.

The entrance on the west side was excavated and found to be a simple gap with a causeway 10 feet wide. No evidence of gate-posts was found but they may have eroded away. A modern, roughly cobbled trackway passed through the entrance and had eroded away any signs of an older trackway. Just inside the entrance, however, an earlier trackway, contemporary with the earthwork, was found to be separated from the modern track by a thick silt level. The trackway was made of a mixture of freshly mined flints and chalk nodules, some of the flints showing signs of battering that could have been produced by iron-tyred wheels.

A four foot wide trench was cut across the interior of the earthwork from north to south. The stratification was leaf-mould above soft, yellowish loam, above orange-brown clay loam. No structures or post holes were found but two small stake holes appeared at the northern end of the trench. The soft loam level produced potsherds of Belgic character. Only one third of the interior was explored, and no hut structures were located.

Continuing from the earlier trackway was a paved yard, of which 54 X 48 feet was uncovered. This area had a sticky clay overlay and was interpreted as a paved stockyard. Samples of soil from the overlay were examined by Dr I Cornwall, whose results showed that the concentration of phosphate present was not enough to be derived from animal dung, and that there was no evidence of human occupation. These results posed the question as to whether the enclosure was ever occupied; or if it was perhaps an unfinished structure, abandoned for some reason, before the final form was achieved. A small firehole was the only feature in the paved yard, and this has been suggested as a possible camping place of a night-watchman guarding the stock. Some pottery and a few animal bones were found above the paving in the sticky clay, and bones of ox or cow and sheep were found elsewhere on the site.

One hundred and thirty pieces of pottery were found on the site, all of Belgic type, and some Belgic wheel-turned pottery was found to be in use at the time of the construction of the earthwork.

A tentative date of AD 1–50 has been suggested by Mrs M Cotton for the initial foundation of the earthwork and this would be consistent with a Catuvellaunian expansion to the south of the River Thames.

In the early part of this century a lot of excavation was carried out in Cookham by the antiquarian Stephen Darby, who lived at Cookham Dean. Most of this work took place between the year 1902 and 1908 in the areas of Windmill Shaw, Round Coppice and Hillgrove Wood, and are described in Darby's book. He attributes the sites to the latter part of the Prehistoric period, which is probably correct, but was unable to obtain any specific dates for his finds. Mr Darby reports that he found numerous large pits which he considered to be 'pit dwellings', an idea that has been discarded by later archaeologists. It is difficult to put these sites in context and it is probably sufficient to say that he found some proof of early occupation. Aerial photographs show a considerable number of cropmarks in the area of Hillgrove Wood, but these will have to wait until some future date until they can be properly examined.

The Royal Hundred of Cookham

Pits in Windmill Shaw northern end of No. 399. on the Ordnance Map

March 10 1905. Carefully opened up a little trench with a trowel across the bottom of the largest Pit. (No 4.). At a foot below the surface a little to the east of the centre of the pit in a stiff loam the trowels struck against a stone which proved to be a flat ragged flint which with three other similar flints at equal distances surrounded a large smooth pebble; there were some large gravel flints outside these but lying irregularly. On carefully removing them – found some bones beneath

N
Dry Close
Depth in Centre of Pits
No 1 – 7 ft in
2 – 6 3
3 – 6 – 6
4 – 12 – 0
No 1.
No 2.
No 3.
No 4
Dry Close
E
Iron Fence
March 12th 1905.

these were as soft as cheese and could only by very great care be taken up without breaking: most of them were covered by the 5 stones. The bones were a lower jaw bone which lay obliquely with the teeth downwards; thigh bones, rib, loose teeth &c. These Prof. Lydeker was good enough to examine and declared them to be bones of the Bos longifrons

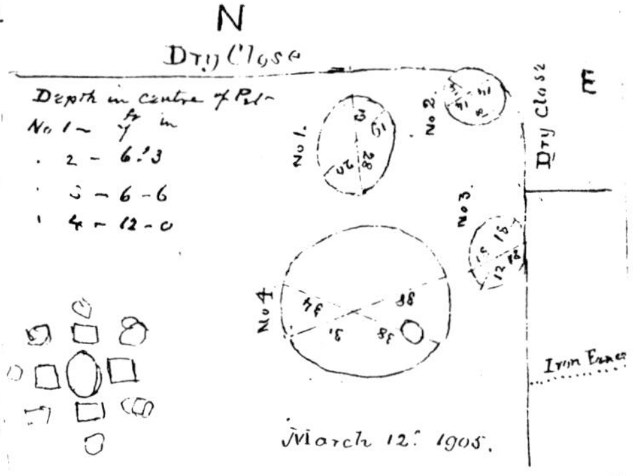

March 27 1905. Examined the other pits. Found in the north westerly one (No 1) the next largest to No. 4. about a foot below the surface under 3 small flints some small pieces of Charcoal 3/4" to 1 in long. The other two pits did not yield any thing

Each of the pits except No. 4 has easy slope upwards towards the west: shewing the entrances to be on the west.

An Extract from Stephen Darby's Notebook c. 1905, Regarding the Examination of Prehistoric Pits at Windmill Shaw.

CHAPTER 3
Roman Cookham

In AD43 the Roman army, under the command of Aulus Plautius, landed on the south coast and after several skirmishes defeated Caratacus and took command of the Belgic kingdom. Britain was then on the verge of becoming Brittania, another province of the Roman Empire. During the next 400 years the Britons were to receive the benefits of better administration, advanced building and farming techniques, improved communications and all other advantages of the Roman way of life. In return, the Romans were to receive an income from the Province.

The Romans built a series of new towns from which to govern the new province, often on the sites of previous Belgic *oppida*. New roads were constructed to link these major capitals, which often appear as straight lines on the map. Lesser roads connected the main roads to rural settlements. The main objective of the Romans was to tap the natural resources that Brittania had to offer, and little interest was shown in developing the countryside. The economy of the countryside, where no natural resources were available, was based on farming and providing supplies of grain, vegetable and animal produce were available, the conquerors did not interfere with the British farmer.

The Middle Thames Valley, including the Cookham area, was entirely rural during the Romano-British era and the pattern of settlement was one of Romanised farms or villas sited by triangulation at one and a half mile intervals. Each villa-farm was an estate in itself and paid taxes to the cantonal capital at *Calleva Atrebatum*, situated at Silchester, south of Reading. There are several known villas in the area, especially on the fertile plain between Maidenhead and Reading, and due to the accuracy of the

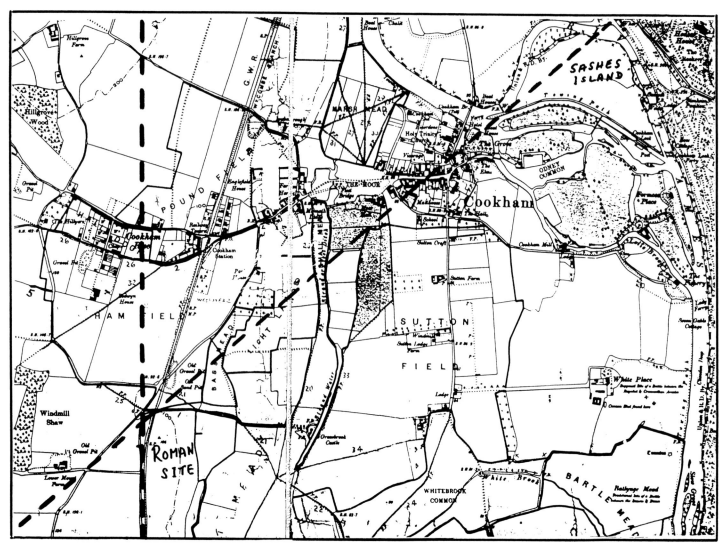

Roman Roads at Cookham

Agrimensores, or Roman land surveyors, sites for the unknown villas can often be pinpoited. One such villa may await discovery near Hindhay Farm, Pinkneys Green, where in 1906 Darby found Romano-British pottery. Nearby, opposite the Pinkneys Green Brick and Tile Works, several other broken vessels were discovered.

Another Romano-British site occurred on Gibralter Meadow, at the foot of Winter Hill. Here in 1906 workmen reported removing 'barrow loads' of pottery which Darby recognised as being Roman. There is not enough evidence to determine the purpose of this site but its position relative to the Thames suggests a possible ferry point. It is a shame that in the early days of archaeology such sites were not properly investigated.

One major Roman site proved by excavation was discovered by the Cookham branch railway line in 1958 at map reference SU.885838. The Belgic occupation of the site was described in the previous chapter, but usage of the area as a Romano-British estate continued for another 400 years. Close by the Belgic enclosure a well of Roman date was found which could be dated to the second century AD. The well contained large quantities of pottery, the complete skeleton of a pig, a wooden writing tablet, and iron agricultural implements, a worn quern stone and a small piece of gold leaf. A piece of Samian ware, manufactured by the Romans in France, was stamped **Sacer**, being the name of the manufacturer. Two brooches and four coins of the Roman period were found nearby and a T-shaped corn-drying kiln, which are usually associated with villa-farms.

Further excavations carried out in 1968 at SU.885841 produced more evidence of this site. The main feature was a rectangular corn-drying kiln, complete with stoke-hole. The kiln was roughly 9 foot square, and built of chalk and flint. During the clearing of the debris from this structure a quantity of tiles of *imbrex* and *tegulae* type were found, which are normally used to roof substantial Roman buildings. This is probably an indication that an undiscovered villa-farmhouse lay nearby. Small finds on the site included a Constantine coin, a penannular brooch and a bronze bracelet.

This site lies at the crossroads of two reported Roman roads which pass through Cookham. The first is known as Alderman Silver's Road, after the person who discovered it, and was located last century before subsequent building made the route obscure. It runs from Braywick to Cockmarsh and was at the time traced along this whole length. Its true destination was probably from Staines to High Wycombe, two known Roman towns. At one time it could be clearly seen from the platform of Cookham railway station.

The second road is of much greater importance and linked the cantonal capitals of *Verulamium* (St Albans) and *Calleva Atrebatum* (Silchester). The route is usually known as the Camlet Way and is registered in the official list of roads as Route 163. The course of the road has been traced by the Viatores group from Verulamium to Hedsor Wharf where it crosses the Thames. The route through Cookham is more obscure but a natural extension crosses Alderman Silver's road near the railway bridge at the end of Whiteladyes Lane, very close to the Roman occupation site mentioned above. Recent theories suggest that settlements regularly occur at Roman crossroads, and the site at Cookham appears to be no exception.

Another theory tested at many sites in Britain and known as the Piercebridge Formula, suggests that where a Roman road crosses a main river this is invariably a river port. When one concedes this point it would seem reasonable that this should occur, as the Romans frequently had to transport stone and other heavy goods and the easiest way to do this would be by water, as the alternative was horse-drawn vehicles which could carry limited weight. The question then arises as to whether such an installation existed at Cookham.

The key to this enigma is Sashes Island, where the line of the Camlet Way suggests a river crossing at Hedsor Wharf. The Thames at this point divides into several streams which would be easier to bridge than the wide fast flowing river. The Lock Cut, which is the main route for boat traffic, was only dug out in 1830 and was not therefore in existence in the distant past. However, during its excavation numerous skeletons, swords and javelins were found together with wooden piles, bones and pottery which at the time were attributed to the Romano-British period, and provided evidence of Roman activity.

In June 1895 an excavation was carried out at Hedsor Wharf by Alfred Cocks, James Rutland and Stephen Darby, after workmen reported finding a wooden floor

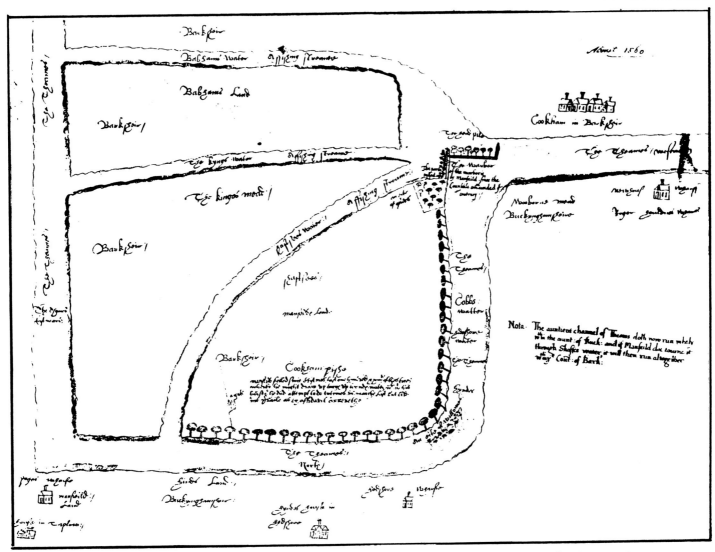

Sashes Island c. 1560 showing lost waterway

supported by oaken and beech piles five foot in length and nine inches in diameter. Up to 25 upright stakes were located indicating a substantial structure which at the time were thought to be supports for pile dwellings, which were in vogue at the time. Several more piles were located in 1969 during levelling operations on the site. Small finds on the site included human skulls, Roman pottery and large quantities of oyster shells often associated with Roman sites.

Later authorities consider that the structure may be that of a Roman bridge carrying the Camlet Way across the Thames and Sashes Island, in which case we might expect to find some indications of a river port. In the majority of cases where these ports occur the Romans had excavated side channels in which to moor their boats for loading and unloading in similar style to a dock. Strangely enough, a map of Sashes Island, reportedly dating to 1560, shows a canal across the island which has since disappeared, although evidence of where it has been filled in, probably from dredging, can be detected on the site.

If Cookham ever was a Roman inland port then it is likely that a small settlement existed there to house the workers from such an installation. Some ports also had small forts associated with them, but in the case of Cookham this is unlikely, although Sashes Island was to become fortified at a later date.

CHAPTER 4
The Saxon Frontier Town

After the Romans left around AD400, the country lapsed into a period of confusion and turmoil, of which little is recorded. The Anglo-Saxons made numerous raids upon the island, before eventually settling and appointing Cerdic, the Saxon chieftain, the first King of Wessex in the year 519. Disorder, war and battle continued well into the seventh century before peace was established, partly with the arrival of Christianity. The Anglo-Saxon Chronicles record that in AD634 Bishop Birinus arrived from Rome and set up his see at Dorchester-on-Thames. In the following year he baptised King Cynegils of Wessex and began his campaign throughout the Thames Valley. Tradition has it that the local people were baptised at the Bapsey Pond at Taplow. By 675 Cookham was part of the Provincia of Sonning and under ecclesiastical rule.

The majority of place names in the Cookham area are derived from the Anglo-Saxon language, and a study of these can reveal a lot ot information on the geographical environment at the time. The Saxons developed the first administrative areas divided into kingdoms and counties or *shires*, derived from the word *scir* meaning 'a part of'. Berkshire or *Berrocscir* was first mentioned in AD860. Each shire was sub-divided into *hundreds* which contained a number of manors which in most cases equate with present day villages and towns.

We are fortunate in that many charters exist to show that Cookham was an important frontier settlement in Anglo-Saxon times. Even today its position on the Thames places it firmly on the border between Berks and Bucks, and in Roman times the river provided the boundary between the territory of the *Catevellauni* and the *Atrebates* tribes. When the Saxons reigned the Thames divided the kingdoms of Mercia and

Wessex with Cookham itself being on the Wessex side. Even then, due to internal squabbles, the settlement was at times under Mercian control. From 670 to 726 Cookham came under the control of Ine of Wessex, but from 726 to 757 there is evidence that Ethelbald of Mercia exercised direct authority. When Ethelbald was murdered in 757 the area reverted to Wessex and King Cynewulf. After Cynewulf was defeated by Offa at the battle of Bensington in 779 Mercia once again took control and held it until the birth of Alfred the Great at Wantage in AD849.

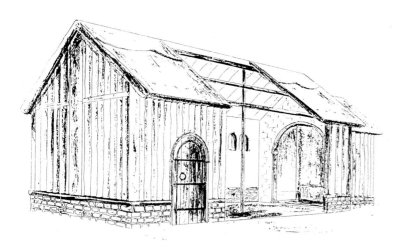

Saxon Church at Cookham AD700

This change of land ownership is reflected in a charter dated c. 798 showing the existence of a monastery in Cookham from the year 700. In essence these early monasteries comprised various communal buildings, individual cells and a church grouped within an enclosure, sometimes linked to a monastic farm. Of the communal buildings a refectory, dormitory and guest house recurred. Some early monasteries, as seems to be the case at Cookham, were 'double houses' for both monks and nuns, ruled over by an Abbess.

The charter reveals that the monastery plus its lands was owned by Aethelbald, King of Mercia, sometime after the year 716. Between the years 740 and 757, when Cuthbert was the Archibishop, Aethelbald presented it to the Church of Our Saviour at Canterbury. After the death of Cuthbert in 758, two pupils, Daegheah and Osbert, stole the deeds and gave them to Cynewulf, king of Wessex, who took possession. Archibishops Bregowine and Jaenberht of Canterbury complained about the removal of the deeds both to Cynewulf and to Offa, King of Mercia, whereupon Offa seized the property from Cynewulf after the battle at Bensington in 779, but without the deeds. Between 779 and 798 Cynewulf repented and returned the deeds to Canterbury, during which time the monastery was under Mercian rule. When Offa died he left it to his heirs.

In 798 a final settlement was made by the charter between Aethelheard, the Archibishop of Canterbury and Offa's widow, the Abbess Cynethryth, passing the title. In exchange for the property the Abbess gave 110 hides of land in Kent, 60 hides called Fleet, another 30 in Tenham and 20 in Cray. In all this totalled 220 hides representing 26,400 acres. If there was an equality in the exchange this could have meant that the lands with the monastery may have been represented by the whole of East Berkshire, which covered 218 hides at Domesday.

The site of the monastery in Cookham is unknown, but the possibility of it being located close to the present church, perhaps in the field known as Little Berry, cannot be discarded. The church dates from the early twelfth century but a section of the wall of the chancel suggests Anglo-Saxon work. Monasteries and priories were often located near water for practical reasons, and if this was the case in Cookham then it could be that the buildings were destroyed in one of the Danish raids.

There is a lot of evidence to suggest that the first settlement of Cookham was located away from the river as was the case at Bray. Flimsy wooden Saxon buildings would not have withstood the consistent flooding that the village has been subject to over the centuries. In the last hundred years, and certainly until flood relief ditches were constructed after 1947, there was evidence of an almost annual flood.

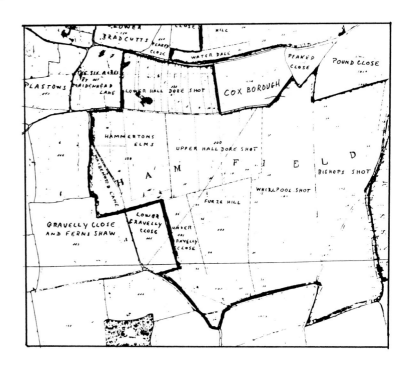

Site of Early Saxon Village at Cookham Rise

Place name evidence suggests that the original Saxon settlement was at Cookham Rise in the area known as *Coxborrow* or *Coxburgh*. The first element of this name *Cox* has the same derivative as *Cook*, whilst the suffix *burgh* indicates a town or borough. The whole has virtually the same meaning as the name Cookham. Adjacent to Coxburgh is

Ham Field being 'the field of the settlement'. A flash flood near High Road in recent years revealed a well which was thought to be of Saxon origin.

Evidence of early raiders on the Thames came from the burials of sixth century warriors in Cookham. The first of these were discovered in 1864 during the construction of the railway between Cookham and Bourne End. The site was located at Rowborough, now a golf course, in a field known as Noah's Ark. There may be some significance in the name as a similar cemetery was discovered at Noah's Ark, Frilford near Wantage. The word *ark* can signify a casket or coffin. At Cookham six skeletons of warriors were found laying on a bed of gravel nine feet from the surface. The burials were pagan and accompanied by grave goods including a sword, two spearheads, the blade of a dagger and three shield bosses. Other weapons are reported to have been found but not listed, the most unusual find being a two-handled basin of bronze.

Another group fo 27 human skeletons were found in a gravel pit in Cookham by a Mr Henry Stubbs, but sadly there are no details of this find. In 1874 when the burial mounds on Cockmarsh, previously mentioned, were examined the remains of a Saxon warrior were found as a secondary interment, an example of the re-use of sanctified ground. The right shoulder of the warrior was covered by a shield boss, and nearby was a pottery drinking vessel, an iron knife and the bones of a dog and a sheep.

The Anglo-Saxon Chronicles record numerous raids by the Danes in the ninth century commencing with the battle of *Acleah* in 851 when they were defeated by King Ethelwulf. In the years 870/1 they had more success when they took Reading for a short period but were driven away. In 1006 they went up river as far as Wallingford and sacked the town, and continued their harassment for five years from 1009 to 1013 during which they took Oxford.

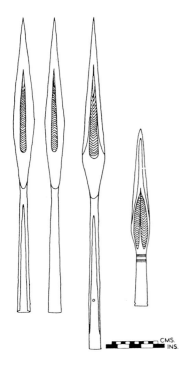

*Danish Spearheads
from the Thames*

Throughout this ordeal settlements along the Thames were destroyed and their valuables seized. As a measure against the invaders Alfred the Great carried out a review of his *burhs*, or defended settlements, which was issued as the *Burghal Hideage* document during the years AD911–9. The document lists all the *burhs* in

Wessex previously in existence together with additional forts erected before 892 to ensure that no part of Wessex was more than twenty miles from a fortified centre. One of the new forts was listed as Sceaftesege, and was situated on Sashes Island at Cookham.

Identification of the *burh* location as Sashes Island comes from place names. The name *Sceaftesege* derives from *Sceaf* (a personal name) and *ege* (an island), the whole meaning 'Sceaf's Island'. Sceaf was the first legendary king of the House of Cerdic, who according to Anglo-Saxon legend, was born in Noah's Ark, yet another mention of this biblical boat. It is known that the name *Sceaftes* always changes to *Shaftes* by the twelfth century, as happened in the town of Shaftesbury. The form *Shafseies* is found on a brass in Cookham Church which is dated 1577. In an assize roll of 1241 nine people are accused of having disseised Henry de Mora and his wife of Moor Hall of a free tenement in *Shaftesya*. In the document the land in question is described as an island 22 by 33 yards, presumably a piece of land cut off by a rivulet, within the larger island of *Shaftsey*. There are many other variations of this name which eventually changes to *Shawses* (1609) and then to Sashes.

+ Here lyeth the body of Raffe More Gent' who married Mary the daughter of John Babham, Esq. He purchased Whiteplace Bullocks and Shafseies and other lands in Cokeham and dyed without issue of his bodye on the feast day of St. James the Apostle in the yeare of our lorde God 1577.

It is likely that the fort at Cookham was completed by the year 886, and fell into disuse after it had performed its defensive function. The *Burghal Hideage* document gives us details of the fort and its garrison of men. The length of the palisade which would have been required to enclose the *burh* was 1375 yards which would have enclosed about half of the 54 acres of the present island. Any excavation of the fort on Sashes Island would be hampered by the fact that spoil from the building of the Lock Cut in 1830 and subsequent dredging has buried any remains to a depth of six feet.

Apart from the documentary and place name evidence, numerous finds in the area substantiate the existence of the fort. When the Lock Cut was made human skeletons and weapons of Saxon origin were revealed. Dredging of the river by Sashes Island in 1856, 1860, 1931 and 1958 provided a series of Danish weapons dropped into the Thames during skirmishes and a Danish winged battle axe was found by the mill

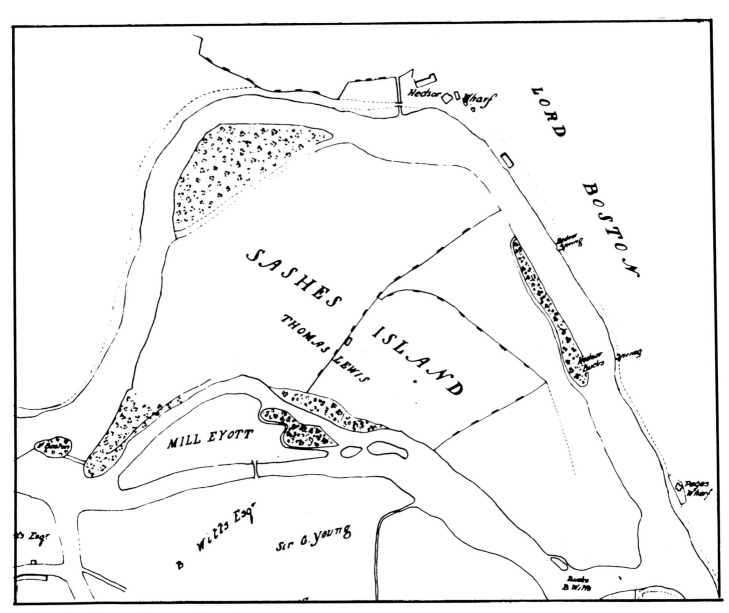

Sashes Island, Site of the Fort of Sceaftesege

wheel in 1896. On the Bucks side of the river an extensive Saxon burial ground was located near Bourne End Station which may have been where many dead warriors were laid to rest.

Cookham became a royal manor sometime between 965 and 975 when the will of Aelpheah, the *shire reeve,* or sheriff of Berkshire, records that he left his lands at *Coccham* to his royal lord, King Edgar. At this time the King was living in his palace at Old Windsor and administering his lands from there. Cookham remained Crown property until 1818.

A charter of the following king, Ethelred the Unready, dated 996 records a meeting of the Witan, or Saxon government at Cookham. The meeting was to confirm the will of Aethelric of Bocking, when his widow had presented a heriot of her deceased husband. The outcome of the case is of no great importance but it is interesting to note that it was attended by 1 Archibishop, 3 Bishops, 2 Aldermen and 3 Abbots as well as numerous lords who were West Saxons, Mercians, Danes and English. Such a gathering of important people suggests that a small palace or a governmental building existed in Cookham to accommodate these meetings.

With a monastery, a fort and perhaps a royal meeting place it would seem that Cookham was an important settlement in Saxon times; perhaps ideally centrally situated in border country. At a later date its importance was to fade but not without leaving its mark.

Saxon Fort on Sashes Island

40

CHAPTER 5
Medieval Development

The late Saxon town of *Coccham* probably formed a nucleus around the present church in the area shown on the map as *Little Berry*, whilst the later medieval settlement extended as a linear development each side of the High Street and encompassed the larger field designated as *The Berry*. The name Berry derives from *burh*, as do *bury, burgh* or *borough*, and describes a medium sized settlement. Medieval Cookham was restricted from extending to the east by the moor which was constantly flooded by the Fleet Stream. The causeway crossing the moor is likely to be of ancient origin and provided an escape to higher ground.

Anglo-Saxon rule in Britain came to an abrupt end in 1066 with the death of Edward the Confessor. The English throne was seized by Harold, Earl of Wessex, even though it had been promised to William, Duke of Normandy. This move led to the Norman invasion in August of that year, and the Battle of Hastings where Harold was slain. The Duke appointed himself William I of England and moved into the palace at Old Windsor. In 1070 he built Windsor Castle to defend the Thames, which in the year 1110 replaced the palace at Old Windsor as the royal residence.

After 20 years of his reign William laid down plans for the Great Survey of England, which when completed became the Domesday Book. He instructed his Barons and churchmen to compile lists of their land holdings together with details of resources and manpower. Accordingly, a full list of manors in each shire was prepared and presented to the King in 1086. From this information he hoped to keep a tighter rein on the annual taxes owed to him by his tenants.

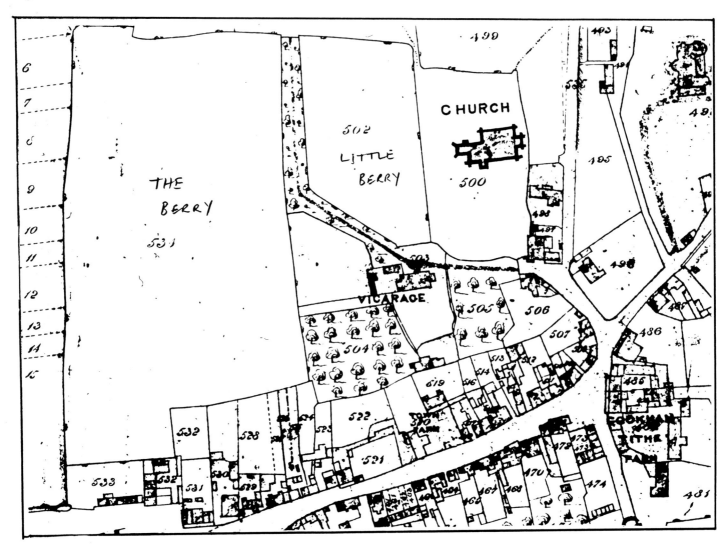

Cookham showing the location of The Berries

The Causeway

43

The Domesday document was written in medieval Latin, and today remains the earliest available gazetteer of towns and villages in England, listed as boroughs and manors. The document is not perfect and has some discrepancies depending on the literacy of the clerks appointed to prepare it, but nevertheless provides a starting point for any historian studying the origins of a settlement. The entry for the manor at Cookham, spelt *Cocheham* translates as follows:

"Land of the King in the Hundred of Beynhurst, King Edward held it. Then 20 hides, but it never paid tax. Land for 25 ploughs: 32 villagers and 21 cottagers with 20 ploughs, 4 slaves; 2 mills at 22s 6d; 2 fisheries at 13s 4d; meadow, 50 acres; woodland at 100 pigs; the other half is in Windsor Forest; from the new market which is now there 20 shillings.

Value of the whole before 1066 £50; later £? 50s; now £36; however, it pays £45.

Of these 20 hides, Reinbald the priest has 1½ hides from the King in alms, and the church of this manor with 8 cottagers and 1 plough; meadow, 15 acres, value 50 shillings. Two other clerics have ½ hide of it and 2 cottagers with 2 ploughs; meadow, 8 acres, value 5 shillings."

An analysis of this entry tells us a lot about Cookham as it was in 1086 and before. King William I held it in *demesne*, or as a royal manor. At this time Cookham was situated within the hundred of *Beynhurst*, which takes its name from the settlement of Binfield. Before 1066 it was held by Edward the Confessor and was 20 hides in size, which in modern terms is 2400 acres, or the equivalent in hectares. The settlement never paid tax, presumably because it was a royal manor. There was enough arable land to require the use of 25 ploughs.

The work force included 32 villagers or villeins and 21 cottagers, which were less affluent peasants. These were heads of households so to calculate the population the total is normally multiplied by an average of four, which makes a total of 212 people. In addition to this there were 4 slaves working on the manor. The above work force had 20 ploughs with which to work their land.

Of the manor resources there were 2 mills with an annual income of 22 shillings and 6 pence; both situated on the Thames. The river also provided 2 fisheries valued through the eels it produced at 13 shillings and fourpence. There were 50 acres of meadow which probably equated with Widbrook and Cockmarsh, and enough woodland to feed 100 pigs on acorns and beech mast for one year, which may have been the wood now known as The Hockett.

The entry states that the other half of the woodland 'is in Windsor Forest'. These were the areas of Binfield and Sunninghill which came under the control of Cookham manor, and later formed part of the Hundred of Cookham. The entry also lists a new market valued at 20 shillings for which permission was presumably granted by William I, as there was no recorded market during the time of the Saxons. The likely position of the market square was probably on the edge of the moor opposite the Crown Inn.

The value of the manor before 1066 was £50, reducing to £36 by 1086, perhaps due to destruction caused at the time of the Norman Conquest. However, it would seem that the Lord of the Manor actually received £45.

Of the total of 20 hides, Reinbald held $1\frac{1}{2}$ hides (180 acres) from the King in alms, and the church of the manor. This churchman is normally referred to as Reinbald the Priest, and his role at Cookham was one of Rector, as indeed he was for 30 other churches. He is said to have been the King's Chancellor and Dean of the College of prebendaries at Cirencester, and as such probably only made rare visits to Cookham. Reinbald's holding at Cookham was situated at Can(n)on Court, reflecting the Canons of Cirencester, although the name is now misspelt. Similarly his holding at Bray was at Canon Hill. His lands extended up towards Cookham Dean where numerous fields were listed as church property. On his holdings he had a work force of 8 cottagers with 1 plough and 15 acres of meadow which was valued at 50 shillings.

Cannon Court Farmhouse

The entry tells us that a further $\frac{1}{2}$ hide (60 acres) was held by 'two other clerics', with 2 cottagers, 2 ploughs and 8 acres of meadow valued at 5 shillings. These 'clerics' were probably churchmen, and may have been priests in charge of small chapels at Binfield and Sunninghill. In a Domesday entry for Burnham Hundred it is recorded that *'Reinbald the Priest holds 1 hide from the King in Boveney, which lies in the lands of the Church of Cookham'*, which suggests that Cookham had control over the small Norman church of St Mary Magdalene, now closed, which is sited close to the Thames near Boveney Lock. After Reinbald's death and when St Mary's Abbey at Cirencester was completed, Henry I granted all his holdings, including the church and rectory at Cookham, to the Abbey in 1132. This was confirmed by John and stayed in their possession until the dissolution in 1547.

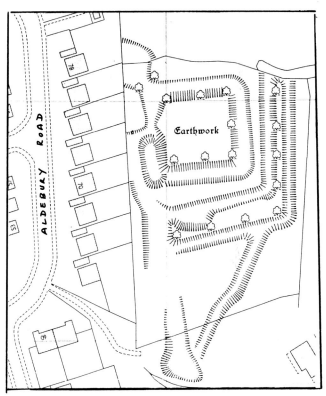

Whilst the Domesday manor of *Cocheham* covered a majority of the land later known as the Hundred at Cookham, there was a further smaller manor centred on North Town, which was to herald the beginnings of Maidenhead, a town formed in the thirteenth century on its present site. The Domesday entry read as follows:

"Giles, brother of Ansculf, also holds Elentone. Siward held it before 1066. Then and now for 3 hides. Land for 4 ploughs. Two men, Hugh and Landri, hold from Giles; they have 2 ploughs; 6 villagers and 4 cottagers with 1 plough.

Meadow 16 acres; woodland at 10 pigs. The value was 60 shillings, now 40 shillings."

An analysis of this entry works on the same principles as that of Cookham. Giles, brother of Ansculf was a tenant-in-chief to the King and a Norman Knight whose family name was De Pinkney. Their name derives from the French town of Picquigny on the river Somme, and it is from this family that Pinkneys Green gets its name, a point which will be

*Elentone Earthwork
at North Town*

Boveney Church

discussed further in another chapter. Before the Conquest the Saxon lord Siward held the manor.

It was a small settlement taxed at 3 hides or 360 acres, with arable land for 4 ploughs, 16 acres of meadow and woodland for 10 pigs. The population as mentioned number 42, and as Giles was undoubtedly an absent landlord, the manor was sub-let to two men, Hugh and Landri. Its value was 60 and then 40 shillings.

We are fortunate in that we know a lot about this small manor. The name *Elentone* is perpetuated in the housing estate Ellington Park off the Cookham Road, and it is close to here at the bottom of Aldebury Road that the manor house was sited. It is represented by a moated earthwork which was excavated between 1966 and 1972 and co-directed by the author. The earthwork was square and surrounded by three moats which had long since silted up. An examination of the central platform, which had been constructed of earth from the moats to raise it above the flood level, revealed a Norman longhouse with flint and chalk foundations and wooden door lintels. The building had one main room with sub-divided sleeping quarters at one end. In the centre of the room stood a hearth built of tiles on edge which would have been used to heat the whole building.

Outside the house was a paved yard and stable where large quantities of horseshoes were found. The kitchen quarters were a separate area, no doubt for safety reasons, and when this complex was examined a whole series of earthen floors was excavated showing an occupation over a long period. Two wells, and an industrial area were also located on the platform. Some two tons of pottery were collected during the excavation, and metal objects representing every facet of medieval life.

Some of the pottery used at the Norman manor house at Elentone was manufactured at Pinkneys Green. During the digging of foundations for the Sterling Homes estate in the Camley Gardens area in 1964, eleven pottery kilns were unearthed on the site which proved to be a major medieval industry. A catalogue of the manufactured wares

CAMLEY GARDENS 1964

*Medieval Pottery
Kilns at Camley
Gardens*

from these kilns is still in preparation, and there is no doubt that they were distributed over a wide area. The types of vessels were mainly domestic and included cooking pots, pie dishes, skillets, pans, pitchers and storage jars. Magnetic dating of the pottery provided a date of the early 13th century for the earliest extending perhaps into the 15th century.

Throughout the medieval period and until the dissolution in 1547 a percentage of the land and resources belonged to Religious Houses. Foremost of these was the Abbey of Cirencester which took over the lands and the church previously held by Reinbald. The right of the ferry belonged to the Abbot who also had special rights of pasturage in Widbrook, and on Cockmarsh where he grazed his pigs. The Nunnery of Little Marlow held 2 acres of land in Cookham on a moated site on which they housed and fed their animals. Both the Abbots of Chertsey and Waltham held 5 acres in the field known as *West Mede*, and the College of Shottesbrooke held another portion. The monks of Bisham had a grange close by the church at Cookham Dean, and land at the base of Winter Hill in Stonehouse meadow.

By 1166 the original manor of Cookham was broken up by sub-infeudation into several smaller manors which were held by many of the local gentry. There were six notable estates formed of which the manor of *Lullebrook* was probably the most important. The Odney Club is the site of the original manor house, and another of a similar name existed in Bray. The estate seems to have been formed in part from 120 acres of land in Cookham granted in 1205 to Adam de Burnham, having been

Widbrook

C.J.

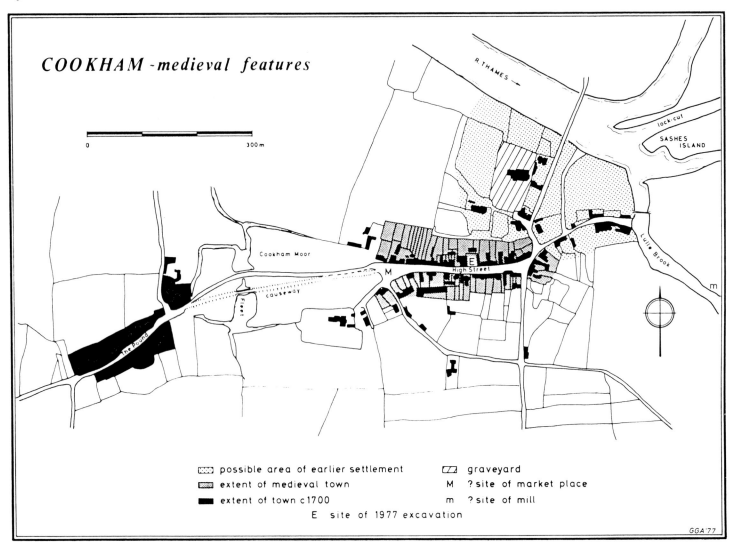

COOKHAM - *medieval features*

possible area of earlier settlement   graveyard

extent of medieval town   M   ?site of market place

extent of town c1700   m   ?site of mill

E   site of 1977 excavation

GGA '77

previously held by William de Buggehesel. Adam's heir sold it in 1248 to Simon de Passelewe from whom it was purchased in 1252 by William, son of Sweyn. The Lullebrook name became attached to the manor when in 1292 it was bought by Walter de Lullebroc. In 1341, when it was described as 140 acres and a weir, it had passed to William Trussell who settled it upon his religious college at Shottesbrooke until the dissolution. In 1547 it was granted to Thomas Weldon who held the manor until 1660.

The manor of *Spencers alias Knight Ellington* evolved from the earlier Domesday site of *Elentone*. The prefix *Knight* is thought to have derived from the Knight Templars, although the earliest tenant, Giles de Pinkney was himself a Norman Knight. The name *Spencers* which was immortalised in the title of Spencers Farm, on which Aldebury Road was built, came from the Despencer family, later owners and ancestors of the Princess of Wales. In the thirteenth century the manor was in the hands of Henry de Elington and William de Coleworth. John le Despencer was holding the manor in 1341 and died in the same year as license was then granted to his widow Margaret for an oratory in her *manse* at Cookham. By 1428 Nicholas Pinkney conveyed the manor to John Norreys, whose family held it until 1616.

The above manor held lands in the area of North Town and Furze Platt. By the twelfth century the family of de Pinkney had formed a new manor called *Pinkneys* in the region of Pinkneys Green and Cookham Dean. Simon de Pinkney held it in 1199 and Henry in 1318. John Pinkney acquired more land in 1411 and Arnold, his son, died in 1430 seised of the 'manor of Pinkneys Place' held by suit at the hundred court of Beynhurst. In the year 1456 the manor passed from the Pinkney family to Robert Beaumont, when it was described as 'six messuages, 300 acres of land, 40 acres of meadow, 200 of pasture and 41 acres of wood which was a considerable holding.

The manor of *Great Bradley* was situated in the Winter Hill area of Cookham Dean, where they were expected to provide a ferry at *Bradelhithe* at the bottom of Stonehouse Lane. The manor was held in 1347 by Herbert St Quintin, and a century later was in the lands of the FitzHugh family, passing to Sir Thomas Fiennes in 1513. The later manor of *Cannon court* evolved from the estates of the Abbot of Cirencester and took on the name after it was granted to Thomas Weldon in 1541. The reputed manor of *Harwoods* evolved in the sixteenth century from land held by the

Lollibrook Manor

Woodmancote family, and the manor house, probably built by the Weldon family, stood on the southern slope of Mount Hill.

Lands along the river by Widbrook belonged to the manor of *Bullocks alias White Place*, now represented by the farm of that name. On the site a medieval dovecote can still be seen and a series of Elizabethan cottages now turned into barns. This was a late manor granted by Thomas Gillot to Ralph More in 1564 for 99 years. By 1700 it was in the hands of the Manfield family.

One further estate which was not recorded as a manor existed at Babham End, now the land on which Formosa stands. The name *Babham* meaning 'Babba's settlement' may have described a separate community in Saxon times, but there is no proof of this. William de Babham, who probably took his name from the settlement, held land in Cookham in 1342 and the family were present there until 1612. There are monuments and murals in Cookham church to the Babhams. The land was purchased by Admiral; Sir George Young in 1794.

The Dovecot

White Place Farm

CHAPTER 6
Cookham Village

To describe Cookham as a village is probably correct, even though in the year 1225 it was described as a borough at the assizes. It may well have taken on the status of a town had it not been for the growth of Maidenhead in the thirteenth century as a town on the main road from London to Bristol. This occurred after a wooden bridge had been erected across the Thames by 1250.

The main building in any settlement, and in most cases the oldest, is usually the church. The Church of the Holy Trinity at Cookham is no exception and was erected in Norman times with additions over the centuries. There is just the possibility of Saxon work on the outer sanctuary wall in which case it may have been part of the earlier monastery that existed there around AD800, or a re-build of the same.

An analysis of the building reveals many additions during the different periods. The church mentioned in the Domesday Book would have been a simple sanctuary linked to a nave, the whole being about 40 feet in length. The building materials were flint and chalk quarried locally perhaps from Quarry Woods at Cookham Dean, with timber and probably thatch. Around 1140 the nave was lengthened by the Normans

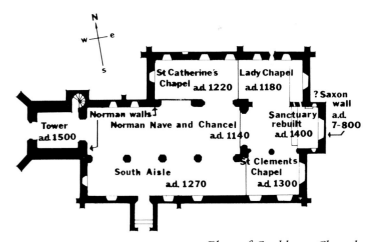

Plan of Cookham Church
(John Brooks)

Medieval grave by Lady Chapel

to twice its original size forming one long rectangular building.

Of the extensions to the church the Lady Chapel was erected by 1182 on the north side, in honour of an anchoress, or hermit, who dedicated her life to the service of God. She lived in a specially built walled-in cell on the sunless side of the church adjoining the sanctuary. It is recorded that Henry II paid this lady a half penny a day from 1171 until she died in 1181, perhaps, it is suggested, to do penance for Henry who was responsible for the murder of Thomas a Becket in 1171. When she died the present Lady Chapel was built on the site of her cell. During recent work on the church a grave of Norman type was located outside the chapel by Ted Sammes of the Maidenhead Archaeological & Historical Society. It is tempting to think this might be the simple grave of the anchoress.

The Lady Chapel was extended on the north side by the addition of St Catherine's Chapel in 1220, built in Early English style. Fifty years later, in 1270, with a steady increase in the congregation, the south wall was demolished and a south aisle added. At this time three internal pillars were erected to support the roof. The final extension was that of St Clement's Chapel in Decorated Style which completed the southern site of the church, sometime around 1300. The sanctuary was rebuilt a century later; and the tower added around 1500.

The church suffered the so called Victorian improvements, which obliterated some of the original work, but otherwise remains a good example of a parish church that has served the community for over a thousand yeras. There are many signs of its chequered past within the church and some interesting memorials. Notably there is one on the south wall to Arthur Babham erected by his wife in 1561, and shows father, mother and their six children at prayers. Another in the nave is a brass to Edward Woodyore

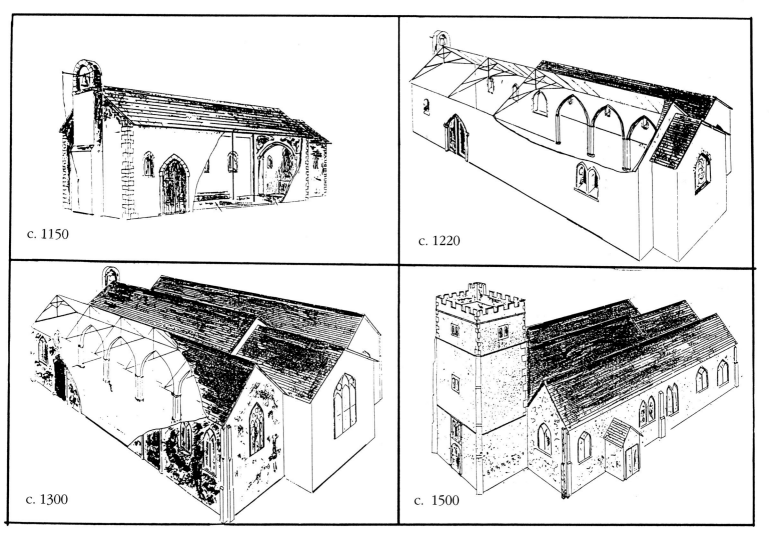

c. 1150

c. 1220

c. 1300

c. 1500

*The Evolution of Cookham
Church (John Brooks)*

Holy Trinity Church

HIS SOVLE DISCHARGD FROM BODIES BVSSIE THRALL
HEER EDWARD WOODYORE WAYTS THARCHANGELS CALL
WHOSE PIETIE TO GOD DEVOVTLY BENT
WHOSE PITT E PRONE TO SVCCOVR IMPOTENT
WHOSE HONEST PLAYNE SINCERITIE OF MINDE
WHOSE NATIVE MILDENESSE TOWARDS ALL MEN KINDE
WHOSE TEMPER LOATH TO GIVE OR TAKE OFFENCE
WHOSE GRATITVDE AS APT TO RECOMPENCE
WHOSE FASHION GENTLE & WHOSE DEALINGS IVST
WHOSE CONSTANT FRENDSHIP & WHOSE FAITHFVLL TRVST
IN LIFE & DEATH MADE WOODYORE TREBEL DEER
TO GOD & MEN & TO HIS LOVING PHEER
WHO (TVRTLE LIKE VNTO HIS LOVE STIL DEBTOR)
INTOOMBD HIM HEER BVT IN HER HEART FAR BETTER
HEE DECEASED DECEMB VII AN SALVT 1615 ÆTAT 59 SHEE MARTII X° AN SALVT 1613 ÆTAT 60

Brass to Edward Woodyore 1613

The Pecke Brass of the Holy Trinity

Brasses in Cookham Church

dated 1613 installed by his good lady, who by some mistake seems to have pre-deceased her husband! The ornate font erected to the memory of Robert Pecke and his wife in 1520 has an inscription which tells us that Pecke was 'sumtyme master clerke of the spycery of King Harry the Syxte'. Also on this font is a delineation of the Holy Trinity, showing Father, Son and Holy Ghost.

The Tarrystone

As one might expect many local families are represented by the tombs in the graveyard, including the Spencer family. A gravestone to Stanley the artist has only recently been erected and lies to the right of the main path. Adjacent to the churchyard is Churchgate House, originally built in the 14th century. In 1595 this was the house of Edward Woodyore, who has the memorial in the church. The building is traditionally known as the one time residence of the Abbot of Cirencester, although as rector of the church he would probably not have visited on many occasions. Renovation of the house in 1993 suggested that it was built around 1350, and produced a priest hole and some 17th century shoes hidden in the ceiling, perhaps to ward off the evil eye.

Facing the High Street on the corner of Odney Lane is the enigmatic Tarrystone. Originally called the Cookham Stone, it was removed from the present spot by George Venables in 1839 when Cookham Bridge was built and taken to Mill House Gardens. The act of removal reputedly brought bad luck to the Venables family and a curse upon their milling business.

The Stone is believed to have been a boundary marker for the lands of the Abbot of Cirencester, and three other similar stones have been noted in the area. In 1506 it seems to have been associated with local sports as the Cookham Court Rolls of that year state that 'the tithingman presents that the warrener ought to hold sports at Cookham stone on the day of Assumption, and he has not done so'. Geologically speaking it is a sarsen stone which is not native to the area.

Churchgate House

63

The Stanley Spencer Gallery

In 1909 Sir George Young rescued the stone from Mill House and had it placed on a traffic island in the middle of the High Street outside the Stanley Spencer Gallery. In 1936, because the island was required for a street lamp, it was moved back to its present position.

The Stanley Spencer Gallery stands on the corner of the High Street and houses the paintings and works of Cookham's most famous resident. The building began its life in 1846 when it was a Wesleyan Chapel, at which Spencer himself worshipped as a child. Eventually it became too small for its congregation and was replaced by a new Methodist Chapel at Cookham Rise. The hall was purchased by Colonel Ricardo who refurbished it and opened it in 1911 as the King's Hall, the king in question being George V. It was given to the village as a reading and recreation room and was used as such until the Second World War. For a period it was used for a multitude of purposes, including an overflow classroom for Holy Trinity School and was opened in 1962 as the Stanley Spencer Gallery. It now houses a permanent collection of the artist's paintings together with other souvenirs of his life, including the battered pram full of painting materials that Stanley regularly wheeled around the district.

The paintings on display include *The Last Supper (1920), Christ Preaching at Cookham Regatta (1953–9)*, which was an Edwardian scene painted near the Ferry Hotel, and *Swan Upping at Cooking (1915–9)* which features the riverbank near Turk's boathouse. Fernley, the house in which Stanley Spencer was born, is further along the High Street and carries a blue plaque.

Cookham High Street is a linear development flanked by a great number of scheduled buildings. The most incongruous of these is Ovey's Farm which looks out of place amongst the bright array of shops, but was undoubtedly built before the town was extended. Originally the building was a medieval hall-house erected in the 14th century and took its name from Richard Ovey, who farmed there in the 18th century. It has been known under a variety of other names which include Cookham Town Farm and Hamerton's Farmhouse. The Methodists used it before their chapel was built in 1846.

Ovey's Farmhouse

The Bel and the Dragon

The Maltings

Hostelries in the High Street are the 16th century Royal Exchange, the Bel and the Dragon and the King's Arms. The Bel and the Dragon, which takes its name from a biblical story, was known as The Olde Bell in 1759 when Martha Dodson of White Place purchased the building from Sir Kenrick Clayton, which had changed to The Bell and Dragon by 1791. It was originally built in the late 15th century and now serves as a small hotel and restaurant.

Underneath the Beefeater facade the King's Arms is a timber framed building dating to the 17th century. During the coaching era it was a stopping place for the coach running from Windsor to Reading, and the arch which led to the yard and stabling is still very much in existence. It was formerly the King's Head, and was the home of the widow, Martha Spott, in 1668 when she minted her own coinage. Her token showed the crowned head of Charles II surrounded by the words 'Martha Spot of the King's Head' and on the reverse 'Her halfpenny 1668' with the words 'In Cookham in Berkshire'. The Spott family can be traced back to 1639 in the village and it would seem that Martha was very much a character. In 1671 she was fined for laying dung on the highway, and again in 1675 she was again in trouble for placing rubbish heap in the street.

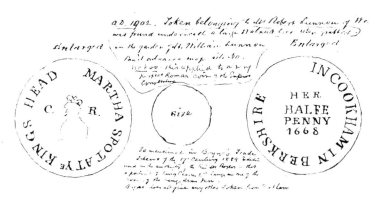

Martha Spott's Token
(Drawn by Darby)

The group of buildings now known as the Brewhouse and Maltings partly in the High Street and partly in School Lane dates back mainly to the 17th century. They are reminiscent of the time when these industries were carried out in the village firstly by Thomas Gibbons, whose premises were on the ground which lies between the churchyard wall and the road leading to the bridge. In 1674 the Malthouse was demised by Thomas Gibbons and was then occupied by John Benwell, maltster. The Ray family purchased the business in 1698 and moved it to the new premises on the south side of the High Street. At first it was a malting business but by 1770 Richard Ray had enlarged the buildings and turned it into a brewery. His initials R.R. can be seen on a plaque built into the wall of the brewery. Abraham Darby purchased the business in 1785 but died in 1801 after which it was in the hands of his sons until they disposed of it in 1837 to Neville Reid's Windsor Brewery. They

Moor Place

The Kings Arms

dismantled the Brewery and enlarged the malthouses, but eventually closed the business in 1906. After that the premises were used for a short while by the G.W.K. Car Company, who manufactured cars between 1914 and 1931.

The Old Forge on the edge of Cookham Moor is a relic of the age when horse traffic was the dominent form of transportation. The building is listed as 16th century but Darby maintains that the house was built by Noah Barnerd in 1617. The Lane family owned it for many years, and James Lane was the smith in 1842. By 1911 Timothy and Ernest Etheridge had taken over the premises, but sold it to Thomas Emmett, who remained as farrier until 1949, when the forge ceased to operate. It is now used as a store by the Forge Motor Company. The Forge House has changed hands numerous times since 1960 and is presently the Cookham Tandoori Restaurant.

In contrast to many of the other buildings in Cookham, Moor Hall can almost be considered as recent. It was built by William Skinner, a London merchant in 1805. When he died it was leased by Stephen Darby, the historian, who was running the brewery. In 1889 the hall was extended with special chimneys designed by Francis Devereaux Lambert, and in 1919 it was purchased by Captain Fodel-Phillips. Odeon Theatres took it over in 1940 and after the war cartoons were made there by Gaumont-British Animation under the direction of David Hand. Since 1971 it has belonged to the Institute of Marketing.

Cookham Moor has featured in the life of the inhabitants since time immemorial, and has been used for numerous events including fetes and fairs and as a cricket ground. At one time the moor was under water at least once a year, and the need for a Causeway to carry traffic across the floods was probably recognised centuries ago. However, the earliest record of a built-up causeway is in 1770 when villagers complained that the seven bridges on Cookham Moor 'ought to be replaced by the Lord of the Manor'. The mention of seven bridges indicates the size and length of the old route. There were frequent complaints about the state of the bridges which culminated with the Great Flood of 1894, but it was some time before the present bridge was erected due to the generosity of Mrs Emmie Balfour-Allen, who laid the stone in 1929.

CHAPTER 7
The Pound, The Rise and The Dean

The causeway across Cookham Moor leads to The Pound, which originated as an enclosure where the medieval Hayward impounded lost and stray animals, and indeed any animals for which their owner had not paid his dues. Judging by the modern name this enclosure stretched from the causeway as far as The Gate public house.

Today The Pound contains an assortment of houses and hostelries which were mainly built from the 17th century as an extension of the village. An exception to this is the Old Pound Farmhouse which is considerably earlier and was mentioned in the will of Roger Austin in 1545. The building has an inglenook fireplace and some old bakery ovens.

Adjacent to the farmhouse is the old Fire Brigade building which was erected in 1910 at the instigation of Colonel Ricardo and Henry Pinder-Brown. The building still has the bell-turret and weather vane. In 1929 it was sold off and a temporary brigade break up took place. After the Brigade was re-instated and numerous temporary premises used, the Fire Station was erected in Berries Road. The 'Sir Roger' was the first motorised fire engine and was purchased from the Maidenhead Brigade for £120. At the full extent of The Pound stands The Gate public house which was built on the site of an older alehouse called The Anchor. In the early stages it was called The Gate Hangs High and the licensee, Luke Maskell, erected a sign which read:

The Gate hangs high,   *Refresh and pay*
And hinders none.   *And travel on*

Pound Farmhouse

74

Cookham Rise, as the name suggests is on a higher elevation than the village itself, which was a good enough reason for the Saxons to have an early settlement there in the area of the Alfred Major Recreation Ground. The area is a natural modern extension of the village, and around 1880 comprised just a few houses in High Road. The main expansion took place as late as 1950–60 with some large housing estates. The railway was in the main responsible for this, as trains became more efficient and fast travel was available to Maidenhead, High Wycombe and London. The station was opened in 1854 by the Wycombe Railway Company, and a branch line from Bourne End to Marlow added later, on which the train became known as the Marlow Donkey. The line from Bourne End to Wycombe was eventually closed in 1970.

There are not too many buildings in The Rise which are worthy of special mention. The Pinder Hall, which has been used for a variety of functions over the years, was erected in 1936 by Captain Henry Pinder-Brown in memory of his wife. The house Spindlewood in High Road has gone down in history as being in the grounds of the Victorian building called Hillyers. This old residence, which for a while housed author Kenneth Grahame, was also a site where Gugliemo Marconi carried out some of his experiments in wireless telegraphy. He is believed to have transmitted between Cookham Rise and Hedsor Hill, a distance of three miles. Marconi stayed at the house as guest of his cousin Dr Leander Jameson somewhere around 1896.

A building now gone which featured in the history of Cookham was Strande Castle, reached along a track from The Rise. It was originally known as Grazebrook's Folly, and stood on Strande Water, known in medieval time as *Le Stond*. It was a castellated building and was erected between 1870 and 1885 by a Mr Grazebrook, an architect who was, by all accounts, an eccentric. The villagers of Cookham certainly thought so and told tales of how he patrolled the battlements with his shotgun and blasted away at imaginary raiders.

The castle is reported as having its resident ghost, a 'grey lady' who was said to have crossed Strande Water and entered the building each night. Although there is little foundation for this apparition, legend has it that a tower stood there in the twelfth century, and leases in the Record Office show that Strande Water is very ancient, and that there was fishing there in the medieval period.

In 1888 Mr Grazebrook erected dams at the castle to hold back the water, and this brought complaints from the villagers who stated that 'the water at Widbrook was far too low for their cattle'. Mr Grazebrook refused to remove the dams and this resulted in the incident known as The Battle of the Strande. On Whit Monday, 1888, 500 men from Cookham and elsewhere stormed the castle and began removing the dam.

While Grazebrook's labourers tried to repair it they were pelted with mud by Peggy, a Cookham man with a wooden leg. A full scale mud-slinging session ensued, which ceased when the mob captured Mr Grazebrook's hat, and tore it to shreds as a token gesture. He was awarded damages in the High Court of October 1890. Between 1900 and 1917 the castle was owned by Francis Lambert. The Ricardo's lived there in the 1920's and Julius Grosscurth during the thirties. Miss Grosscurth was the last tenant and stayed in the building until 1959, after which deterioration took place leading to the demolition of the building in May 1968. The grey lady may, of course, still be resident.

A strange incident occurred in Ham field, Cookham Rise, in 1680 which resulted in a major inquest. John Sawyer and his son were ploughing a field when a violent thunderstorm broke out. A lightning bolt from the storm killed them both and a team of four horses. A pamphlet was issued on this unusual occurrence.

Cookham Dean is one of those settlements which is difficult to define, and has no recognisable pattern of settlement. One tends to think of the centre as being Starling's Green, possibly because the church is there, but it should be remembered that the church was built in Victorian times. Other ancient groups of buildings occur at The Mount, Winter Hill and Dean Bottom and all could have had a claim to being the hub of habitation there. Cookham Dean has its ups and downs, despite the fact that the name is generally thought to have originated from the word *Dene* meaning a valley. The English Place Names Society suggested that it might have derived from the fact that Osbert de la Dene held land in Cookham in 1220 but he is more likely to have taken his name from the settlement. Some other spellings are *Le Dene (1344), Le Deane (1608)* and *Deanefield (1608)*. This latter spelling translates as 'a field or open space belonging to the Dean'. But was the Dean a settlement or a title? One cannot ignore that Reinbald, the Domesday rector of the church, held church lands which

A FULL AND TRUE
RELATION
OF THE
Death and Slaughter
OF
A MAN and his SON at PLOUGH,
TOGETHER
With FOUR HORSES,

In the Parish of *Cookham* in the County of *Berks*, Sept. 2. 1680.

SLAIN BY THE
𝕿𝖍𝖚𝖓𝖉𝖊𝖗 𝖆𝖓𝖉 𝕷𝖎𝖌𝖍𝖙𝖓𝖎𝖓𝖌
THAT
Then and there happened, as may fully be teſtified by credible Perſons, whoſe Names are hereunto adjoyned.

LIKEWISE
The ſame day happened another ſad Accident near *Norwich*, eight Perſons being ſtruck dead in a Church Porch by Thunder.

Publiſhed for prevention of falſe Reports.

LONDON, Printed for *John Harding* at the *Bible* and *Anchor* in *Newport-Street* near *Leiceſter-Fields*, 1680.

*Strange occurrences at The Rise
(1680) and The Dean (1815)*

LINES
WRITTEN ON THE
DEATH OF JOSEPH BISHOP,

Who was Shot by George Smith, in Bisham Wood, October 18th, 1815.

ON EARTH COVER NOT THOU MY BLOOD!

HUMANITY assist me to indite,
My thoughts to flow, my pen to write
A tale too true, in pathetic strain,
Of him who lately has been slain.
At Cookham Dean there liv'd a pair,
Once happy; and devoid of care,
(Save what a family is wont to give,
In these our days, to teach us how to live.)
Bishop by name, well known thro' all the place,
Of manners gentle—and Plebeian race.
Blest with a Partner whose only care,
To see him happy, and his pleasures share:
For years they liv'd free from domestic strife,
That oft alas! pervades the married life,
Till one sad night, by fatal error drawn
From his peaceful cot, before the morning's dawn;
In search of game, the paltry cause,
That reflects disgrace on English laws.
Three wretches at once did him assail,
And nought but blood their sanguine minds avail.
Like tigers on their defenceless prey they flew,
And only life could satiate the infernal crew,

For one barbarian fir'd the murd'rous shot,
Too true the aim !—be died upon the spot.
Too soon the widow found her happiness was flown,
Her children fatherless,—her husband gone.
Struck with sad anguish at the dreadful tale,
Tho' pregnant, down in strong hysterics fell;
Her piercing cries alarm the neighbours near,
Whose soothing language cannot reach her ear.
In vain her frighten'd infants round her cling,
No comfort they afford, no consolation bring.
Her husband's kill'd; in one sad moment torn,
From wife and family; Oh! never to return.
Canst thou, mean wretch! with all thy sordid crew,
Restore that peace which once this family knew?
No never! Oh! thou great God, on whom all things
depend,
Protect the children,—be the widow's friend.
Vengence alone to Thee belongs,
Do thou revenge the widow's wrongs;
And in thy wisdom all divine,
Let justice, and thy mercy shine.

stretched from Cannon Court Farm to The Mount and he held the position of the Dean of Cirencester. However, the riddle of the name may never be solved.

Before the erection of the church Cookham Dean seems to have had a reputation for lawlessness. Gypsies lived on a strip of common by Grubwood Lane, and poached in Bisham woods nearby. If wanted by the Cookham constable they would hastily move into Bisham parish where he had no jurisdiction. The inhabitants, by all accounts, were as lawless as their gypsy neighbours. The settlement was entirely rural, with a number of cottages constructed of wattle and daub with thatched roofs and earthen clay floors. many of the freeholders of these properties did not overburden themselves with work, but put aside a considerable amount of time for activities such as cock and dog fighting, badger baiting and personal quarrels which were always solved by a fight among themselves, no doubt to public amusement.

The constable, who was a local fruiterer, was not averse to joining in himself as his diary showed that in 1810 he fought with Joseph Bishop at Hatches and with B. Pagot in the same place. In 1812 he records that he 'got off clear' for hitting Mary Smith. So it was that the first incumbent of the church, the Reverend George Hodson, who had been a cavalry officer in the Indian Mutiny, took on the task of taming the roughs of Cookham Dean. This, one might say, was Hodson's choice.

The idea of a Chapel of Ease at Cookham Dean was first suggested by the Reverend F Vansittart Thornton, Vicar of Bisham in 1843. The lady of the Manor, Mrs Anne Mary Vansittart, with the consent of the commoners, gave an acre of common land on Stirlings (later Starlings) Green for the erection of a church, dedicated to St John the Baptist. Mr R C Carpenter was selected as the architect and the building comprised a chancel, nave and south aisle with porch and a western turret containing one bell. The money for the church was raised by public subscription, the dowager Queen Adelaide being among the subscribers. A further grant of £200 was received from the Cambridge Camden Society.

The foundation stone was laid on 18th July, 1844 and the chapel consecrated on 15th May, 1845 by Dr Richard Bagot, Bishop of Oxford. A Vicarage was built on a site

St. John the Baptist Church

79

adjoining the church in 1855 on land donated by Mr H M Skrine, and a Lych Gate, recently rebuilt, erected in 1882.

What some may not know is that St John the Baptist is one of triplets. The architect, Richard Cromwell Carpenter, using almost the same design, went on to build two further churches. The first was the church of the Holy Innocents, built in convict country in Rossmore, Australia in 1847 and the other is St John the Baptist in Buckland, Tasmania which was completed the following year.

*Roof of new lych gate at
Cookham Dean Church*

Starlings Green owes its name to the property adjacent to the Dean church which was variously spelt as Stirlings and Sterlings. The name derived from the house built by Henry Alexander, the fifth Earl of Sterling, whose family originated in Scotland and settled in Binfield, a part of Cookham Hundred. He moved to the Dean after his marriage to Elizabeth, daughter of Sir Edward Hoby of Bisham Abbey. The Abbey had owned the land for some centuries, and at one time there was a Grange on the site which was associated with the religious house.

After the dissolution in 1547 Sir Philip Hoby acquired the land and his nephew, Peregrine, built a house there in the 1660's, which at that time was known as Dyars. The Earl of Sterling moved into the premises in 1690 but the house had disappeared by 1850. Cookham historian, Stephen Darby, built another house on the site in 1880 but this too was demolished in 1975 to make way for a group of new houses. The author was one of a group of archaeologists who explored the site prior to building. It proved to be a complicated excavation due to the continuous habitation of the site, but the foundations of the Sterling House, which had previously been explored by Darby were revealed. Perhaps the most interesting find was the flint and chalk footings found beneath an 18th century stable block, which may have related to the medieval Grange.

There are many interesting buildings and lanes in Cookham Dean which are too numerous to mention. Near the top of Dean Lane is Herries School, formerly Mayfield, where Kenneth Grahame wrote 'The Wind in the Willows'. At the bottom of the lane stands an attractive group of buildings which are all scheduled and are the nearest thing to a medieval manor set-up. These include Dean Farm, the Forge and Forge Cottage, Reddaways, Telford and Cromwell Cottages and Old Solomons.

The Forge dates back to the time of Queen Elizabeth I and is said to have been the home of Richard Warner in 1558. It has been in the hands of David Matthews family for some generations and has had many smiths over the last 400 years. The attractive thatched Cromwell Cottage is a wattle and daub building and is thought to have been a billet for Roundhead troops in the 17th century. The Dean Farmhouse is now a private house, the last farmers being the Jordan family.

The Pound, The Rise and The Dean

Church of The Holy Innocents, Rossmore, Australia

Winter Hill, with its fine views of the Thames and Marlow, is at one end of the Dean. Gibraltar and Stonehouse Lanes are the steep routes leading to the river below. The original Stone House was built by the monks of Bisham, who held the meadow there. After the dissolution it was given by Henry VIII to Anne of Cleves, as part of her divorce settlement. She exchanged it for a manor in Suffolk, and it fell into disrepair. The ruins of the first Stone House were dismantled and used to build a second of the same name, which was patronised by Thames bargemen, and at one time housed an

Cromwell Cottages

C.J.

The Dean Forge

C.I.

83

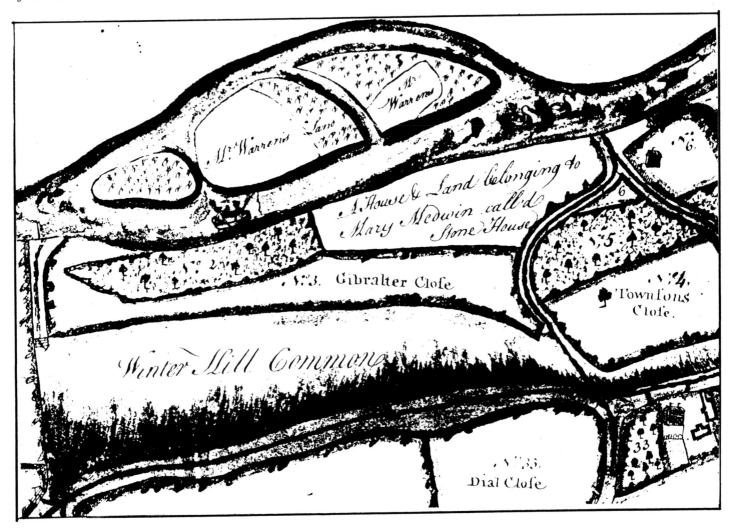

Winter Hill in 1744
(Richardson)

illicit distillery. This house, in turn, was pulled down and the materials used in the building of the church of St James the Less at Stubbings. There is now a third building further east which carries forward a name which has been in use for perhaps five hundred years.

The original causeway on Cookham Moor (printed by Elizabeth Fanshawe before 1835)

Palmers Mail Coach passes Maidenhead Thicket 1784

CHAPTER 8
Pinkneys Green, Furze Platt and Stubbings

Mention has previously been made of the Pinkney family who held the manor of *Elentone* at Domesday and subsequently gave their name to the settlement of Pinkneys Green. From the two brothers, Giles and Ansculf, who came to Britain in 1066 with William I, a dynasty evolved which was later to provide the Earls of Dudley. The stronghold of the Pinkney family was in Northamptonshire, where today the name is perpetuated in the settlements of Moreton Pinkney and Weedon Pinkney. The family owned numerous manors in many counties and it is doubtful if many of them ever visited Pinkneys Green, except in the early days. However, there is a brass in Cookham church commemorating the death of Arnold Pynkeny in 1402.

The development of Pinkneys Green, and indeed of Furze Platt, did not take place until 1890, with the expansion of Maidenhead. The area as we see it today bears no resemblance to the large tracts of common land that had remained untouched from medieval times. The handful of buildings that were in existence before 1800 were merely to house the resident hayward and his gatekeepers who administered the common land for the Lord of the Manor.

To understand the evolution of Pinkneys Green it is necessary to discuss the origins of Maidenhead Thicket of which it was a part. This vast now largely overgrown area formed the southern boundary of Cookham Hundred. It was laid out in the 12th century by the Norman kings as an integral part of the Forest of Windsor. By 1225 the Seven Forest Hundred had been set up and in 1260 one general court was formed to look after the whole forest and ensure uniform administration for an area with royal game and creatures of chase.

By 1321 the rights of the common people to remove wood from the thicket were properly recognised. In an inquisition held in *Elentone* in that year before the Constable of Windsor, it was stated that 'all tenants of the manors of Cookham and Bray since time immemorial have their profits of all open spaces and groves in the said manors within the boundaries of the Forest of Windsor – to wit La Thickette and Bigfrythe. Tenants have housebote, haybote and fuel with common pasture for all animals'.

The Crown left the day-to-day running of the forest areas to the various landholders. Each area appointed a woodward, an officer whose job was to look after the woodlands and function as a forester and a gamekeeper. In 1500 a forest return lists 19 woodwards in Windsor Forest, of which 8 covered the area of Maidenhead Thicket. From this it can be deduced that the Thicket was once a much larger area, and this is borne out by the words of the antiquary Leland who passed through Maidenhead in 1538. After leaving the town he stated that 'for two miles the road was narrow and woody; then came the Great Frith, a wood infested with robbers some five miles in extent'. This would indicate that the Thicket extended past Knowl Hill into Hurley and Wargrave parishes.

The *Frith* as mentioned by Leland is the earliest name given to the Thicket and simply means 'wood or wooded country'. In the Assize rolls of 1284 the 'Thicket of Cokeham' is mentioned. In 1370 it is styled 'Le Thikket by Maydenhythe'. In a lease dated 1606 it is divided into two areas and quotes the Thicket as being 160 acres abutting on the south to a wood called Altwood and being south of the Henley Road. To the north of the Henley Road it was known as the Nockett and extended for 70 acres to Pinkneys gate. Nockett indicates an oak wood, and this is confirmed in 1609 by the use of the name Oaken Grove, which today lives on in the road of the same name.

The Thicket was reduced in size at the time of the enclosure, and in 1859 a man complained that this action was 'to the great undoing of the poorer sort' who were unable to get wood for their Christmas fire. In the 1939–45 war, 64 acres of land were requisitioned, ploughed up and cultivated, which made it even smaller.

The Waggon & Horses

The Thicket was a haven for footpads and rogues for many centuries and as early as 1255 the Henley Road was widened to combat the element of surprise. Robbery was particularly prevalent during the coaching era when travellers refused to cross the Thicket by night. At this time the Henley Road followed the route of St Mark's Road, St Mark's Crescent, Farm Road, and across the Thicket where it came out by Stubbings Church. When the field by Pinkneys Drive is ploughed the tell tale marks of the old road can still be detected.

There is a story of how the Vicar of Hurley was regularly stopped when he visited Maidenhead Chapel, and was paid danger money for crossing the Thicket, of which he was relieved on the return journey! Another recounts how an ostler at the Sun Inn, Maidenhead, held up coaches and then sympathised with his victims when he heard their story at the inn. In 1736 the situation was so bad that Thomas Darvill, landlord of the Bear Inn, Maidenhead, was ordered to pay £20 for information leading to the arrest of any highwayman. With the practice of Hue and Cry in Elizabethan times, whereby all in a hundred were liable to pay if criminals were not caught, the Hundred of Beynhurst was exempt from collective liability for crimes committed on the Thicket.

In this context Pinkneys Green emerged as an area of common land within the boundaries of the Thicket, albeit that the area of clearance was not as large as it is now. Animals, mainly sheep, grazed within its limits, and all roads were gated to keep animals in and unauthorised vehicles out. These were all manned by gatekeepers, employees of the manor. Pinkneys House Gate, also known as Jimmet's gate, was located on the Marlow Road by Clarefield Court and Pinkneys Farm. Jimmet was the last gatekeeper and he travelled from Cookham Dean daily on a barrow drawn by a moke. He had a small gabled hut by the gate, in which he amused himself by making baskets from rushes that he had collected on the common. The gate to the west of the common, near the Robin Hood and Golden Ball public houses, was called Randall's or Hutton's Gate. Hutton was the gatekeeper and had a lean-to up against William Randall's Smithy, a business that was there for many years. Butler's Gate, which was manned by Granny Butler, stood on the Cookham Dean road past the brick kilns and separated the Pinkneys Green Common from the Bigfrith, where the swine were pannaged.

Pinkneys Green had no natural centre and was barely a settlement until the 1890 expansion. From Pinkneys House Gate fields stretched as far as Maidenhead, and from the stile outside the Waggon and Horses as far as Highway, where the fields attached to the farm of that name, which was owned by the Headington family. All the buildings erected at Pinkneys Green were on land categorised as manor waste, that is to say land which had no useful agricultural purpose. That is why today we find groups of houses mainly centred around a public house, as in the case of the Waggon and Horses, the Stag and Hounds, and the Golden Ball. The latter group developed after the opening of the brick kilns.

The alehouses are mainly 19th century, although some may have developed from private houses of an earlier date. The Waggon and Horses stood at one edge of the Green and for over 50 years was managed by John Musselwhite and his son Jack. The Shoulder of Mutton, which once stood in the middle of the Green has now disappeared. At one time the landlord, Mr Brain, sold bread, cheese and ale for fourpence to the agricultural workers. When Mrs Massingburg took over she put a notice above her door reading 'All ye who enter here leave strife behind'. This is strange really, as she is reported to be a prominent member of the Temperance Movement. The Carpenters Arms is another alehouse mentioned in 1854 which seems to have vanished.

Of the larger residences in Pinkneys Green, Clarefield Court is perhaps the best known. The present house dates from the 1890's, but there was at least one earlier residence on the site which many consider to be the main manor house. In 1830 when Thomas Hassey owned it it was called Pinkneys House, but the name had been changed to Clarefield Court by 1854 when it was owned by Edwin Blackburn. Henry Norsworthy rebuilt around 1893 and sold it to Gilder Caledon in 1899. The Litkie family owned it from 1903 to 1931 when it passed to Sir Horace Boot, a local surgeon, who gave his name to one of the wards in St Luke's Hospital.

Ditton House, on the Marlow Road, is probably late Georgian, and the earliest traced owner is Mrs Brant in 1830. By 1854 it was owned by Lord and Lady Lee who held it for the rest of the century. Lee Farm and Lee Lane take their names from the family

Clarefield Court

Stubbings Church

who owned the land in the area. From 1903 for half a century the house belonged to the Garcke family. Emil Garcke helped to start the first bus company in the area.

The old scout hut which stands close to Ditton House originated as a small chapel, linked to Cookham Dean church which was built by Mr Lee to meet the needs of the people living in Pinkneys Green in 1860. A curate was employed to hold the services and look after this part of the district. Lady Lee supplied an altar cloth in 1895 and Mr & Mrs Norsworthy supplied another plus a lectern and Bible in 1899. However, the use of the chapel was discontinued in 1900 and it was turned into a library and reading room. In 1929 it was enlarged by Emil Garcke and used for the boy scouts. In the second world war, with additional evacuees, it was in use as a school.

Scout Hut, Pinkneys Green

The industry that brought prosperity to Pinkneys Green, and resulted in the expansion along Golden Ball lane, was that of Bricks and Tiles. The geology of the area was such that rich deposits of brickearth was available, and this had been realised perhaps as early as Tudor times. Names like *Kiln Meadow* and *Kiln Platt* occurred at Bigfrith, and a packhorse bell located there in 1887 and dated to the time of Queen Elizabeth I was perhaps proof of this. Certainly by 1800 a family named Stevens were working there. Eventually they established a brick making and lime burning business in premises adjoining Ditton House, but this was purchased and disposed of by the owner of the house.

About 1825 the Pinkneys Green Brick & Tile Works was established by Charles Cooper, who built up the business until it was employing 150 people from Pinkneys Green and Furze Platt. His son, John Kingdom Cooper, was well known for his

Brick Kilns

terra-cotta tiles and gargoyles, examples of which can still be seen in many districts of Maidenhead including Laburnham Road, Furze Platt Road, Ray Park Avenue and the Fisheries. Queen Anne House, which stood at the base of Castle Hill, was said to contain samples of all the terra-cotta products including a bust of J K Cooper himself.

Until 1870 the pug mill was worked by horses, and then by steam. In January 1906 a fire destroyed one third of the works and caused £20,000 worth of damage. Perhaps because of this only tiles were manufactured there from 1909. In 1919 it was sold for £20,000 to a consortium who issued shares to the value of £75,000 and renamed it the Maidenhead Brick and Tile Company. Sometime in the 1980's the works were closed down and the area redeveloped.

At the most westerley part of Cookham Hundred is the small settlement of Stubbings astride the later Henley Road. The origin of this name is not known with certainty, but the suggestion is that is was 'the place of Stubs', indicating that a number of trees had to be cut down to form a clearance in the Thicket. The earliest record seems to be when Stubbings House was erected in 1756, and a Mr Cambler, a councillor at law lived in it. It was purchased by Elisha Biscoe who lived in it until 1790, when it passed to Guy Carlton, the first Baron of Dorchester. The Baron had distinguished himself by being the quarter master general in 1759 under General Wolfe at Quebec. Later he became the Governor General of Canada.

By 1808 the house had been acquired by Colonel Brotherton of the lancers, and by 1830 had been purchased by Henry Skrine, of Warleigh Manor, near Bath, for £12,000. Mr Skrine was Lord of the Manor of Cookham for a period and was the founder of the church of St James the Less at Stubbings. The church was built by Silver and Sons, of Tittle Row, in 1849 and was consecrated in 1850. Mr Skrine had obtained land from G H Vansittart of Bisham Abbey on which he also built the school, vicarage and 'Camley Cottage' where John Penny, parish clerk and sexton lived from 1861 to 1921. The first vicar at the church was the Reverend Wadham Huntley Skrine, the son of the founder.

Henry Skrine died in 1853 and his widow in 1866, and their tomb is inside the church. After the Skrine dynasty Stubbings House was bought by Lawrence Wethered, who had an interest in the Marlow Brewery, and was related to one of the best known

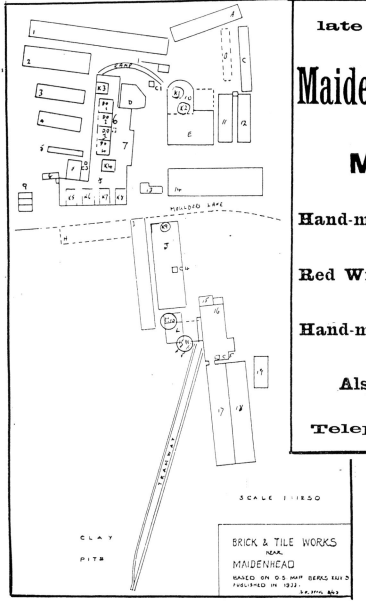

BRICK & TILE WORKS
NEAR
MAIDENHEAD
BASED ON O.S. MAP BERKS XLV 3
PUBLISHED IN 1933.

SCALE 1:1250

CLAY PITS

MOULDERS LANE

TRAMWAY

The Brick and Tile Works at Pinkneys Green

97

Stubbings House

vicars of Hurley. By 1897 the house was in the possession of the Crocker family and then the Smiths who were still there in 1943. During the second world war the house became famous for being the hideout of Queen Wilhelmina of the Netherlands, who had a contingent of Dutch soldiers billetted nearby on the Thicket.

Development of the settlement of Furze Platt commenced around 1874. Before that it had been a rural area with common land similar to Pinkneys Green. The Platt itself was a small triangle of overgrown waste where furze was collected as firewood by the local inhabitants and hence the name. The first roads bounded this triangle and were Marlow Road, Switchback and Cannon Court Roads.

Certainly by 1887 the village was considered important enough to have its own church which was erected as a Mission Church responsible to the Mother Church of St Luke's. It was known as the Iron Church and sufficed for 11 years before any move was made to replace it. In 1896 it was felt that a new and enlarged building was required. The construction of the present brick building dedicated to St Peter was begun in 1897 by Silver & Sons and the church was consecrated on 14th April 1898. The building was enlarged to its present size in 1908.

Most of the buildings in Furze Platt are relatively modern. The local pub is the Golden Harp which dates to 1889 and appears to be named after an important racehorse of that year. The Laundry, which was there for so many years, was started by Mr Edwin Rogers during the 1880's, and the Memorial Hall was opened in 1922.

Eventually Furze Platt became an extension of Maidenhead when the town expanded, but not before owning its own small railway station.

St. Peters Church, Furze Platt

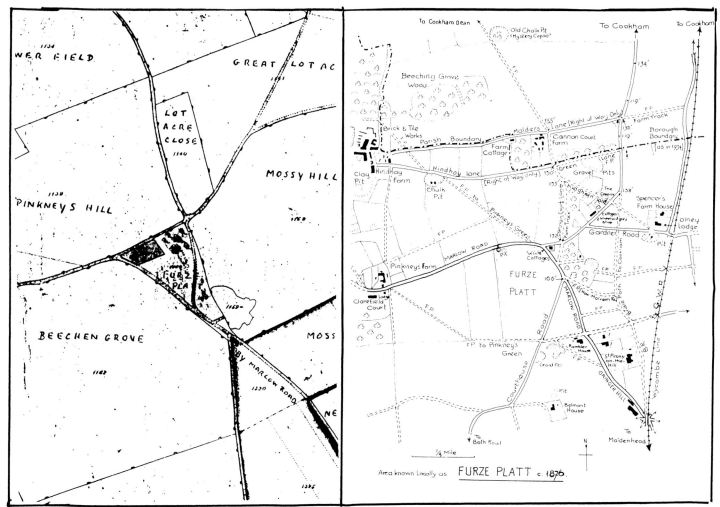

Furze Platt in 1840 and 1876

Craufurd College, now demolished, which stood on Gringer Hill, Furze Platt

CHAPTER 9
Binfield and Sunninghill

Although situated well away from the principal town of Cookham, the settlements of Binfield and Sunninghill were part of the Royal Hundred of Cookham. They were both within the Great Forest of Windsor, and as such probably supplied the manor of Cookham with wood for building purposes and meat or game when the monarch issued a licence for hunting.

The origins of Binfield are to be found in Anglo-Saxon times when the settlement was called *Beinfeld*, a name which translates as 'the open land where the bent grass grows'. Later spellings include *Benetfeld (1160), Bentfeld (1241)*, and *Benefeld (1380)*. Binfield does not have its own entry in the Domesday Book but the Cookham entry informs us that part of the lands were in Windsor Forest. Both Binfield and Sunninghill had chapels that were annexed to the minster church at Cookham which were administered by priests, under Reinbald of Cirencester.

The first named priest at Binfield is Walterus, Presbiter de Benetfield who occurs in a document dated before the year 1162. By this date the church had passed into the hands of the Abbey of Cirencester.

The use of the name Benetfield occurs after 1160 and by 1230 a family had adapted the title when Henry de Benetfield is recorded as holding the manor. Between the 13th and the 15th centuries the manor was part of the dower of the Queens of England, who also had interests in Cookham. A smaller manor in Binfield was held by John de la Beche in 1328 and for his manor house and 120 acres of land he paid four shillings and eightpence rent every three weeks to the manor of Cookham.

Binfield Dec.r 7 1816.

30 **John Constable R.A. (1776–1837)**
Binfield Church
Pencil
4½ × 7¼ ins
Inscribed 'Binfield/Oxfd' and dated Decr.7.1816
Verso: Drawing of a memorial inscription 'JB (monogram) 1665';
also inscribed 'An Essay'

Provenance: From a sketchbook probably owned by
Archdeacon John Fisher, Constable's close
friend.

Literature: Ian Fleming-Williams and Leslie Parris, *The
Discovery of Constable*, 1984, pp. 189 & n.,
191.

Constable executed this drawing towards the end of his
honeymoon, while he and his wife were staying at Binfield (near
Reading) with the Cooksons, parents-in-law of the Rev. John
Fisher. The Fitzwilliam Museum, Cambridge, holds another
Constable sketch (formerly in the collection of Isobel Constable) of
what is evidently Binfield Church, dated 9 Dec. 1816 (repr. Harold
Day, *Constable Drawings*, 1975, pl. 56, and Arts Council, *John
Constable, R.A. 1776–1837*, no. 19). For other Constable drawings
taken during his honeymoon see Graham Reynolds, *Catalogue of
the Constable Collection at the Victoria & Albert Museum*, 1960,
pp. 108–111.

The Church of All Saints, Binfield, is here seen before the
extensive alterations of the late 1840s and 1850s.

The parish church of All Saints dates back to the 15th century, and replaced an earlier chapel which was given by Henry I to the Abbey of Cirencester, as indeed were all of Reinbald's possessions. In 1226 Henry III granted to the church a piece of ground for making a courtyard. Only the font remains to suggest the existence of a church before 1500 to which period the chancel, nave, south chapel and south aisle belong. The south chapel is slightly later in date than the south aisle of the nave, and the tower was added at the end of the same century. The north aisle of the nave was added in 1848, and eleven years later the north chancel aisle was built and the vestry added. The building has been very fully restored, so that few of the windows retain their original stonework.

There are many large residences in the parish with similar names which include Binfield Court, Binfield Park House, Binfield Lodge, Binfield Manor and Binfield Place. The last named is probably the oldest and dates from the reign of Henry VII, though much altered and reduced in size. Of the original building only the eastern wing survives.

John Dancastle bought the manor of Binfield from the Crown in 1595 and thereafter created a dynasty which continued until 1754. It would seem that there were at least four John Dancastles, the third having a memorial placed in the church at his death in 1680. The fourth John resided in the manor house during the reign of George I and was a great friend of the Binfield poet Alexander Pope.

Pope was born in 1688 two months before the Glorious Revolution and came to Binfield in 1700 when his father, who had a sizeable fortune, bought a 20 acre estate in which to retire and pursue his favourite hobby of gardening. This estate was later known as 'Popes Wood'.

Pope was a Catholic, and as such was excluded from public careers, that being the climate of the time. Nevertheless he was fortunate in gaining the friendship of Sir Edward Trumbull, who lived in the nearby Easthampstead Park, and with whom he took daily rides in Windsor Forest.

Alexander Pope

Popes Manor

In 1712 he published his celebrated poem The Rape of the Lock, which caused a minor scandal in Berkshire. He left Binfield in 1716 but not before completing From Windsor Forest which expounded the beauties of the area. Pope died in 1744, having lived through the reigns of five monarchs. Today the residence occupied by Pope is known as Pope's Manor and has been greatly extended. It is a red brick Georgian building and is now the offices of Bryant Homes.

The first eminent person known to have spent his honeymoon in Binfield was William Pitt who bought the manor from the last John Dancastle in 1754. Pitt was the first Earl of Chatham and was later to be known as William Pitt, the Elder, a statesman, Prime Minister and Lord Privy Seal for England.

Pitt has perhaps never been equalled as an orator or a leader of Parliament. In addition to these attributes he was a great minister of war and a master of world strategy. He was the type of man to use in the time of a national crisis, and steered Britain through the Seven Years War when the British were sheep without a shepherd.

'I know that I can save this country and that no one else can' he had boasted. This he did and won the trust of the middle and lower classes who referred to him as the 'Great Commoner'.

It was he who built the house that we know as Binfield Manor today, and landscaped the gardens and lakes to suit his own tastes. It is said that he spent £36,000 on the mansion which was completed in 1754 for his new wife Hester, the only daughter of Richard Grenville of Wotton Hall, Bucks, whom he married. Pitt had three sons and two daughters, the second son being William Pitt the Younger, a great statesman like his father. Pitt the Elder died in 1778 at which time the family sold the house and moved elsewhere.

The manor house was sold by Pitt's nephew to Buckworth Herne who passed the title to William Coxe. The next owner was George, Lord Kinnaird, who bought it from Coxe in 1787 for £10,000, a bargain even by 18th century standards. While Lord Kinnaird held the manor the historian and controversialist, Catherine Macauley Graham, moved into the parish after completing the first volume of Mrs Macauley's

Binfield Manor

History of England. Married twice, Mrs Graham was described by Mary Shelley as 'a women of the greatest abilities that this country has ever produced, endowed with a sound judgement and writing with sober energy and argumentative closeness'. She believed that all men were equal and her belief naturally included women.

In 1795 the manor passed to Claud Russell. During his occupancy Binfield had a famous visitor in the person of the artist John Constable, who also spent part of his honeymoon in the village. Constable had married Maria Bicknell at St Martins Church and then started his honeymoon in Weymouth with his friend, the Rev. John Fisher, who had performed the wedding ceremony. After a six week stay he moved to Binfield where he lodged with his friend's parents-in-law, the Rev. William Cookson and his wife. Cookson was rector of Binfield from 1804 until 1821, and had been tutor to William Pitt the Younger.

During his stay at Binfield, Constable made two sketches of the church. At this time his talent still remained unrecognised, and even after completing the Hay Wain in 1821 his earnings were still meagre. In 1822 he painted Salisbury Cathedral for his friend John Fisher, who was then a bishop. This painting too was unappreciated and it was not until after his death that the public acknowledged him as a classic painter.

Claud Russell continued to hold Binfield Manor during the reign of George IV. The rector of Binfield during this time was Henry Dyson Gabell, a distinguished man who had been headmaster of Winchester School. Changes had taken place in the parish with the enclosure of Windsor Forest which commenced in 1817.

The sheer size of the forest necessitated the provision of hunting lodges where the King and his entourage could stop and rest. Binfield was one of these stopping places and the 14th century Stag & Hounds Inn may well have been a converted hunting lodge. Queen Elizabeth I is said to have watched the maypole dancing from this building, and also stayed in other houses in the village, but her mythical reputation for sleeping around is well known.

Outside the inn are the remains of an ancient elm tree, said to represent the exact centre of the forest.

In 1822 William Cobbett visited Binfield and stopped for breakfast at the Stag & Hounds. Cobbett was an essayist, politician and agriculturalist born in Farnham, Surrey, in 1762. He undertook a series of political tours during which he traversed England on horseback, taking in the flavour of cities, towns and villages. On his rides he travelled hundreds of miles, the accounts of which he regularly printed in his paper Cobbett's Evening Post. These essays were later published in a collected form in 1830 as Rural Rides, which ranks today as a minor classic. A leading journalist concerned in the movement for parliamentary reform, Cobbett tended not to pull any punches when describing conditions in late Georgian England.

While on his travels he drank no wines or spirits and ate no vegetables, contenting himself mainly with bread, milk and water.

During the Victorian era the manor of Binfield passed from Claud Russsell to Sir F Wilder, whose widow sold it to Mr Kinnersley. In 1896 the manor house and 60 acres were sold to Lord Arthur Hill. It changed hands again in 1907 when it was purchased by Lestocq Erskine.

Today Binfield retains its identity as a country village, serving also as a dormitory area for the ever growing town of Bracknell and the citizens of silicon valley. It has seen its share of eminent people, and will no doubt see more in the future when they take their place in the history books.

Today Sunninghill still gives the appearance of a forest area and has not been subject to the same clearance as Binfield. Being close to Windsor Castle it has always been associated with royalty, and developed as a residential area of wealthy people. Early spellings of the name occur as *Sunigehill (1185), Sunninghull (1191)* and *Sondynghill (1447),* which translate as the 'hill of the Sunningas'.

The Stag & Hounds, Binfield

111

The people of the *Sunningas* had their centre at Sonning, and at one time their province took in the whole of East Berkshire. A mention of this tribe is made in an early charter of AD964.

Norman Arch at Sunninghill Church

The small town at Sunninghill is modern in relative terms and the oldest building by far is the church of St Michael and All Angels. This was erected between 1120 and 1130 and consists of a chancel, north vestry, south chapel, tower, and a nave with north and south aisles. It was entirely rebuilt in Perpendicular style in 1807 and 1827, with the chancel, vestry and south chapel added in the year 1888. To all intents and purposes it is now Victorian in appearance, but retains one original Norman door.

When the church was built it was apparently standing on its own with no attached settlement. This is possibly why the responsibility of its upkeep was given by King John in 1200 to the nuns at Bromhall Priory. The Benedictine Nunnery had been founded around 1150 and was situated on rising grounds near Sunningdale.

In 1228 the king issued his mandate to Jordan, the forester of Windsor, to give full access to the prioress and nuns of Bromhall to the 100 acres of waste which the king had granted to the convent, in accordance with the bonds and divisions laid down by the king's courts. In 1231 the king pardoned the nuns the pannage fees due to the crown for 36 pigs, and ordered the agisters of Windsor Forest henceforth to permit the priory to have free pannage. Later in the same year Henry ordered the constable of Windsor to grant the prioress three beams of timber in Windsor Forest, to make shingles for the repair of their refectory, and also to give her an oak. The prioress and nuns of Bromhall obtained licence from the king in 1283 to enclose with a small dyke and a hedge sufficiently low for the entry and exit of the deer, the 100

Old Sunninghill Church before 1827

acres of land which they had of the king's gift within the forest of Windsor, and which they had brought into cultivation.

In July 1285, an inspection and confirmation of the charter of Henry de Lacy, earl of Lincoln, and Margaret his wife to the nuns of Bromhall, was granted by Edward I. By this charter the priory obtained 100 acres of the waste of 'Asserigge' which lay between 'Pillingbere' and the high road from Bracknell and Reading.

The seal of
Broomhall Nunnery

The Priory was dissolved at a very early stage in October 1522 and its possessions transferred to the master, fellows and scholars of St John's College, Cambridge.

The first mention of Sunninghill being a manor in its own right was in 1362 when it was purchased by John de Sunninghill and his wife, Joanna. There was no actual manor carrying the name and the Lords of the Manor seemed to have lived in different residences within the area. The earliest mention is a Tudor mansion called *Eastmore* which seems to have stood on the site at the present Silwood Park. Other ancient mansions in the area included Sunninghill Park and King's Wick.

Fort Belvedere was built in the 18th century and enlarged in the reign of George VI. In 1930 it was taken over by the Prince of Wales and was the focus of attention on 10th December 1936 when the Prince, who had been proclaimed King Edward VIII abdicated in favour of Mrs Wallace Simpson.

The ultimate expansion of Sunninghill as a small town was due to the development of the Wells and Ascot Racecourse. It was in the 17th century that health giving spring water was discovered in the vicinity. Soon Sunninghill Wells became as noted as Tunbridge Wells, Buxton and Bath, and in its heyday attracted royalty. The 'Wells' inn stands today on the site of the original spring which was covered over in the 1970's.

Ascot races, now an annual event in the society calendar, was started by Queen Anne who watched the first race in 1711.

Old Silwood House

The Wells

CHAPTER 10
The Riverside and the Ray Estate

The Thames at Cookham divides into several different streams. One branch encircles Sashes Island passing Hedsor Wharf whilst another is the channel for boats passing through Cookham Lock, which was mainly dug out around 1840 when the lock was built. A third channel leads to the weir and another, anciently known as Lollibrook Stream, encircles Odney Common turning it into an island. This complicated system of waterways probably made it easier to cross the river at times when it was flowing fast.

There was no road bridge linking Cookham with Bourne End until 1840, when the first wooden construction was erected by Freebody. In the early days this was probably intentional to stop raiders crossing from one territory to another. Even then the wooden bridge soon rotted at the water line and the existing iron bridge replaced it in 1870. A toll booth was erected on the Bucks side of the bridge and was the home of a keeper until 1947, when the gates were removed and the river crossing becamse free of charge. In 1980 the Toll House was made a listed building and four years later it was restored.

Toll Booth, Cookham Bridge

Before the bridge there was a ferry which crossed from where the Ferry Inn now stands to Sashes Island. This vital link, which carried livestock as well as people, dates back to medieval times and perhaps even earlier. The operation of the ferry was in the hands of the

The Royal Hundred of Cookham

John Turk is as much a part of Cookham as the Tarrystone. He was born in the village and attended Holy Trinity School before going on to Borlase School in Marlow. From 1963 to 1993 he held the position of Her Majesty's Swan Keeper, and spent 30 years looking after the welfare of the birds, proving himself to be the most colourful character on the Thames. The office had been with the Turk family for 71 years, since John's father, Mr. Frederick Turk, was appointed by George V in 1922. Each year John took command of the swan-upping ceremony during the third week in July, when the new cygnets were marked according to their ownership. The ceremony dates back some 500 years when most gentry, monasteries and boroughs had their own swanmark. Today only the Queen, the Vintners Company and the Dyers Company own swans, which are those situated on the Thames. The earliest appointed Swanmaster was Thomas Gervys in 1355, and today's ceremony is more of a traditional than a practical nature. David Barber, of D.B. Marine at Cookham, has now taken over the duties of Mr. Turk, and holds the title of Her Majesty's Swan Marker.

Brooks family for many generations, who lived in Ferry Cottage alongside the bridge. The ferry finally closed down in 1956. Previously there had been an earlier crossing at Babham, where a pack horse route ran down from Cliveden. This was more commonly known as My Lady Ferry.

Cookham Mill at the end of Mill Lane is the only surviving example of three mills mentioned in the Domesday Book. There was one between the head pile below the Ferry and Shawses Bridge, which was lost when the Lock Cut was excavated, and a second on Ray Mill Island, which will be discussed later. Cookham Mill probably equates with the third which was stated in 1483 to be on Lollibrook Stream, or Babham End Water. This was originally a flour or grist mill, but later went on to produce paper.

The earliest date we have for paper production is 1752 when John Monday appears in a rating list. By 1786 it was in the hands of William Venables, whose family manufactured paper for over 100 years. In 1909 the disused mill was sold to Sir George Young, of Formosa Place, for the use of his son. By January 1910 some of the buildings were being demolished and machinery removed. The mill was eventually turned into homes and in recent times has been used as a recording studio.

The 65 acres that comprise Widbrook Common now come under the National Trust, but have been common land for pasturing animals and collecting fuel since time immemorial. It was certainly so in 1272 when the rector of the church, the Abbot of Cirencester, had the rights to pasture his cattle there. Queen Elizabeth I granted the common in trust to the inhabitants of Cookham and James I tried to lease them out but was unsuccessful.

The Common lies each side of the Lower Cookham Road, and grazing on it has always been strictly controlled. In 1650 it was closed from the beginning of Lent until 3rd May, and from then until Lammas Day on 1st August inhabitants had to pay 6 pence for every cow, 8 pence for a horse or ox, and 4 pence for a bullock or colt. After Lammas Day grazing was free. Nowadays the grazing is from 1st May to 31st October. A toll cottage at the Cookham end of Widbrook housed the gatekeeper who opened

Cookham Bridge

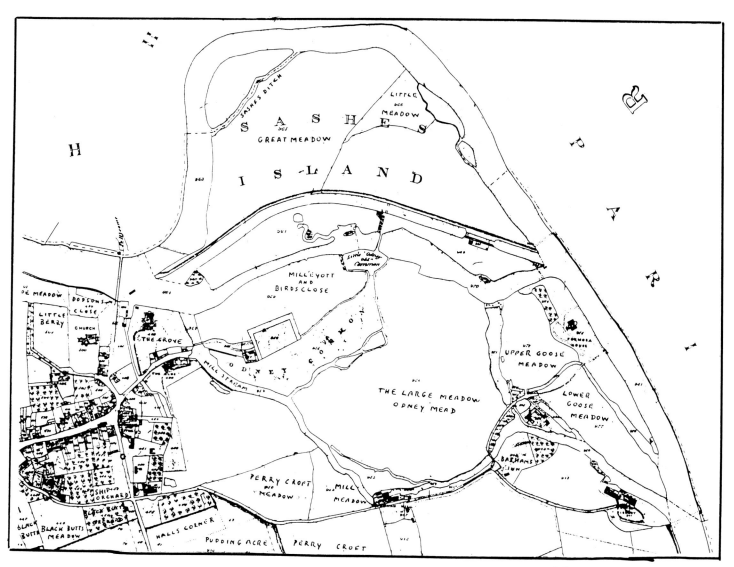

Odney Common and Sashes Island with Field Names

the gates to let animals onto the Common, and travellers off it. The land was handed over to the Maidenhead and Cookham Commons Preservation Committee in 1934.

Widbrook takes its name from the stream that flows across it which is also known as the Whitebrook, but should more correctly be called the Withie-brook after the willows that grow along its banks. There was no road across the Common until 1920, when the increasing number of motor vehicles demanded access at which time Widbrook was divided into two parts.

White Place Farm stands on the north side of Widbrook Common and in medieval times was the site of the manor house of White Place or Bullocks. In 1703 the land belonged to John Dodson, but eventually passed into the hands of the Leycester family. Waldorf Astor, who was living at Cliveden House on the other side of the river, bought the Leycester estate in 1893 and built the present farm house, some out buildings and the half-timbered gatehouse in Sutton Road. He kept a herd of prize Ayrshire cows and housed them in the very elegant cowsheds that he had specially built, which ensured that the beasts lived in better conditions than those in the farmhouse.

A field adjacent to the farm has the name of *Bartle* or *Batlynge* Mead and was traditionally thought to be the site of a battle between the Saxons and the Danes. A mound thought to be an ancient tumulus was opened last century and found to contain remains of 14th century pots, possibly from an old dwelling. Nearby is another spot where the Roundheads and Cavaliers are supposed to have fought, based on the fact that a cannon ball was dug up there.

It was during the Anglo-Saxon period that most of the Cookham fields were given names. Whitebrook Park was situated in the field known as Lower Southey. This together with Upper Southey (ie higher land) made up the island of Southey. The name is derived from Sutt or South = South and Ey = eyot or island, the whole name meaning South Island. Lying south of Cookham village, this piece of land was bordered by the Thames and the Whitebrook stream, and a now silted up ditch forming a true island.

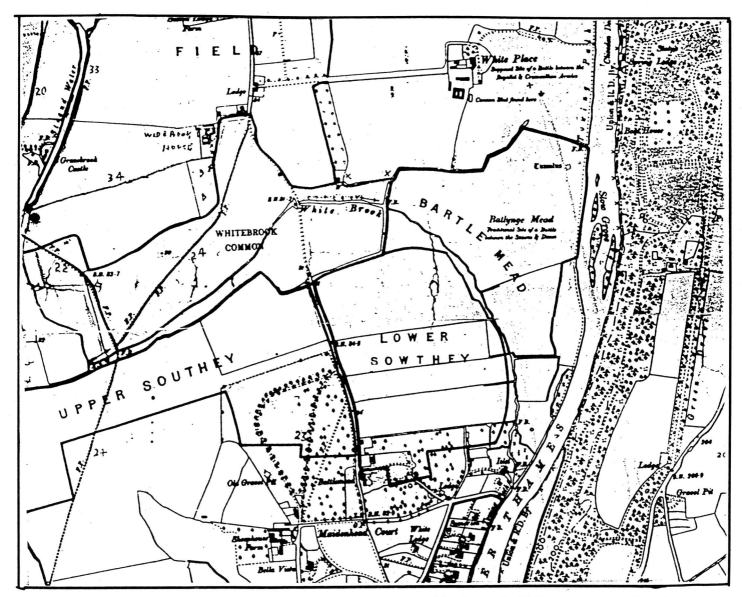

The Saxon Field Names near Widbrook Common

Lower Southey Field was an area of 69 acres as shown in three surveys made in 1609, 1840 and 1845. In 1609 the land was divided into five plots, which, by 1840, had become the four main plots of Sydenham Mead Furlong, Lock Mead Furlong, Middle Shot and Cross Shot which in turn had been split into 45 strips of land for cultivation. In the Enclosure Award of 1845 it was converted into five horizontal plots which belonged to different owners including G H Leycester of White Place Farm and the University of Oxford.

By 1880 the majority of the land belonged to Sir Charles Gervaise Boxall, and it was from him that millionaire Edward Wagg purchased the land to build the Islet Park Estate. It was bought in nine parcels of land which were conveyed between the years 1887 and 1909. it was a large area stretching from the Lower Cookham Road over to the Thames and the confluence of the Whitebrook. Landscaping of the estate began in 1891, but the Island mansion, complete with boathouse on the Whitebrook, was not completed until 1895. To a certain extent the estate was self-sufficient with a dairy (Pine Lodge), a Home Farm, also known as the Bull Pen, and a herd of cows.

Entry to the estate could be made via the West Lodge on the Lower Cookham Road, built in 1900, or the South Lodge in Islet Road. The cedar walk, still in existence, was laid out in 1898 and ran into the estate from the West Lodge. The road linking the south Lodge with the mansion was known as the Drive and was constructed at an earlier date. The Stable and Water Tower on Lower Cookham Road was built in 1903 and undoubtedly accommodated carriages as in 1912 Albert Daubeney, the coachman lived in West Lodge while the gardener Daniel Philips was residing in the South Lodge. By 1936 the Stable was called the Islet Garage.

Islet Park Water Tower

Edward Wagg, known to his family and friends as the Laird, was the younger of two brothers, senior partners in the City firm of Helbert, Wagg & Coy. He and his brother Arthur sat side-by-side in their office in Threadneedle Street, London. Edward was described as a white-haired gentleman with a slight stoop and short legs, who was interested in history, biography and memoirs. He was a very wealthy bachelor who also owned the shooting lodge of Glenlochay in Scotland. He never married but had a good Etonian friend whom he invited for a weekend visit and who stayed for 55 years!

Evidence of his wealth is reflected in a dispute he had with the Hon. Waldorf Astor, an American senator, who had purchased the estate of Cliveden on the opposite bank of the Thames. Mr Astor was irritated by the gabled roof of the Islet which he maintained was spoiling his view and sent a note to Mr Wagg which read: 'The Hon. Waldorf Astor wishes to know whether Mr Wagg will sell his cottage', to which the reply read: 'Mr Wagg wishes to know whether the Hon. Waldorf Astor will sell his palace.'

Sir Charles Boxall owned the neighbouring estate of Battlemead and on his death it passed to William Boxall, who in 1920 sold it to the Duchy of Manchester, of which the Most Noble Angus Drags, the ninth Duke, was the tenant for life. On the death of the ninth Duke in 1933 the property passed to the tenth Duke who sold it to the Investment & Property Trust Ltd in 1947.

Edward Wagg still owned the Islet Estate in 1930 but shortly after this he died. The whole complex was purchased by Lady Burton, believed to be connected with the tailoring firm, by 1935. Her chauffeur, William Wills, was living in the Stable building, which was then called Islet Garage. By 1939, Islet Park had been divided into two sections. The area near the river, surrounding the mansion, remained residential while the portion off Lower Cookham Road became industrial. About 1947, C S Whitworth purchased the mansion and turned it into the Islet Park Hotel and Country Club.

After the Islet Park Hotel closed the mansion was turned into flats as we see it today, and the old parkland was purchased by a number of owners. The next major stage of development came in 1961 when Landstone Investments bought up the land nearer the river and added it to that of Battlemead. Three new roads were built – Battlemead Close, Islet Park and Islet Park Drive.

Islet Park

One of the local names that many people wonder about is that of Ray; which is prolifically used in the river area and prefixes at least a dozen street names. Between Boulters Lock and the bridge there is a confusing maze of Ray, Ray Park, Ray Lea, Ray Mead and Ray Mill roads which make addresses difficult to remember and often keep delivery drivers encircling the area for hours.

All this confusion has to be blamed on a family of yeomen and traders from Cookham who carried the name Ray, sometimes spelt Rey or Rea, which basically means The River. They were major landholders in the Manor and Parish of Cookham, which 100 years ago stretched over as far as Maidenhead Bridge. Their family extends back at least 700 years and in their time they were farmers, millers and brewers.

The earliest mention that we have of the family is in 1304 when John atte Rey (John at the River) had a certain isle and paid an annual rent of sixpence. The isle in question was Ray Mill Island, where at an early date the Rays operated a corn mill. The mill itself is mentioned in a lease of 1348 whereby money passes between 'Nicholas atte Reye to Hugh of Braywick of the Mills called Reye Mulles in Cookham'. At this time the property was described as 'a messuage with six-and-a-half acres of meadows with pools, weirs, islands, fishing pools and winches in Cookham'. The fact that islands is mentioned in the plural seems to be substantiated on a map of 1637 when Ray Mill Island comprises Ray Mill Close and Ray Mill Eyote which were not joined together.

The history of the island is interlinked with that of Boulters Lock and both must be considered at the same time. The word Boulters is not a personal name but derives from bolter, an alternative description of a miller. John atte Rey seems to have been the first miller, and he was followed by Alexander, Nicholas and William. The Rays were associated with the island until at least 1800 even though it passed into the hands of Sir Francis Norreys who sold it to Sir Thomas Bodley in 1608. Sir Thomas used the proceeds from the mills to provide an endowment for the famous Bodleian Library in Oxford.

Boulters Lock first received mention in 1585 when John Bishop lists it as 'Rea Lock' belonging to one Harry Merrye, a yeoman of H M Chamber. At this time it was a flashlock and was situated where the present weir crosses the river. The first hint of its

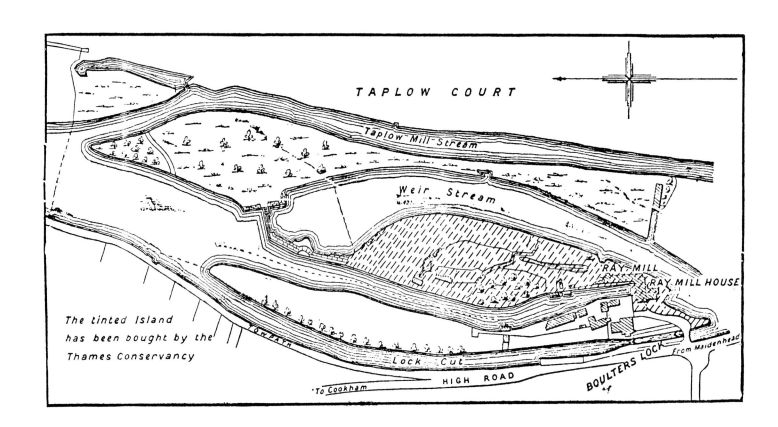

*A Plan of Ray Mill
Island in 1909*

present name came in 1746 when Griffiths wrote of the 'Bolters (or millers) Lock'. However, when the flashlock was replaced by a pound lock in 1772, it retained the name Ray Mill Pound, and was not called Boulters Lock until after 1842.

Richard Ray was appointed the first lock keeper in February 1773 at a weekly wage of six shillings and by 1774 a house had been built for him on the island. He stayed as keeper for more than 50 years and only retired when a new lock and cut were built on the present site in 1829. Richard was the last recorded member of the Ray family to be connected with the island which was purchased by the Thames Conservancy in 1909. The Conservancy demolished Ray Mills but retained the Mill House which is now Boulters Hotel. The lock was rebuilt and opened by Lord Desborough in 1912.

Meanwhile, back in Cookham the Ray family had been carrying out other activities, as evidenced by early wills and monuments in Cookham Church. In November 1549 there was a Gylls Ray who left his money to his son Radoulphe and his two daughters, rather inappropriately named Johne and Cecil. his wife Marget was given custody of the children in the will while his brother Thomas had the use of them, whatever that meant.

There was a David Ray who in May 1612 left the farm called Louches to his son John, and a Giles Ray who in April 1705 left the same farm to his son Giles, together with land called West Mead and a house in North Town. The same Giles Ray, of Pinkneys, purchased a house and land adjoining Cookham Moor in 1698, and left it to his son Robert who carried on a malting business there, while his grandson Richard turned it into a brewery. There are monuments to the last of the Rays in Cookham Church, otherwise their name lives on in the many river roads which were built on the flood plain at Maidenhead during the Victorian era.

Sometime around 1770, perhaps to raise money for the brewery venture, the Rays sold off land to create the Ray Lodge Estate close to Maidenhead Bridge. The estate consisted of a wooded park with a small creek which passed under a rustic bridge and flowed into the Thames. In the centre of the park was the large 18th century Ray Lodge Mansion with a Lodge House on Bridge Road opposite Oldfield Road. The first owner of this building was Sir Isaac Pocock, who with his wife Ann, led a life of

Ray Mill, Boulter's Lock

130

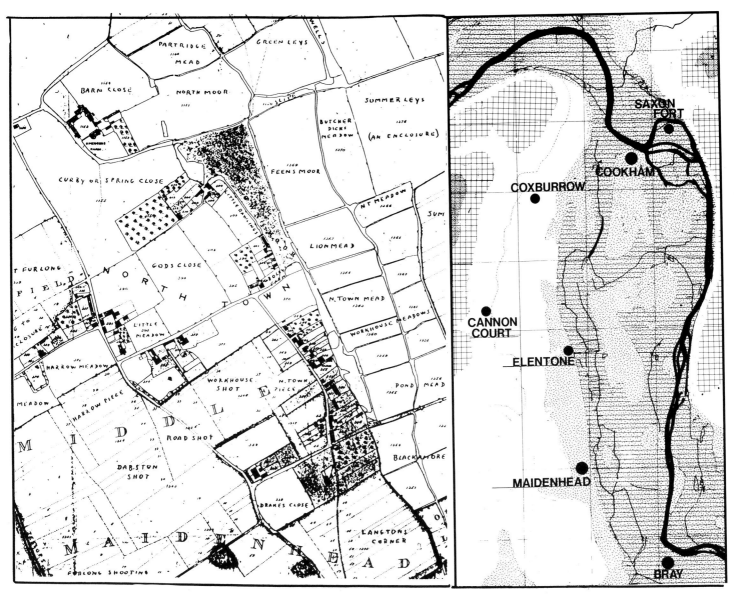

(a) North Town with Field Names 1840

(b) Main Cookham Sites in Relation to the Flood Plain

benevolence. Ann was closely associated with St Mary's Church and presented an organ to the Chapel in 1817. Sir Isaac was drowned in the river near his house in 1810 and Ann passed away in 1818 after leaving enough money to endow a school and weekly dole of bread to be provided by Marks, the High Street baker.

Sir Isaac's brother was Nicholas Pocock, the famous marine painter who died in 1821, but it was Nicholas's son Isaac who inherited Ray Lodge from his uncle in 1818. Isaac was Deputy Lieutenant and a JP for Berkshire, as well as a painter and dramatist. In 1807 his picture, Murder of Thomas A'Becket, was awarded a prize of 100 guineas, after which he painted an altar piece for St Mary's Chapel. He also wrote many dramas several of which were adaptations of the Waverley Novels. he died at Ray Lodge in August 1835. Memorials to all the Pococks can be seen in Cookham church.

For a while Isaac's son, Isaac John Innes Pocock, a barrister, stayed on in Ray Lodge and then moved into Bridgewater Lodge on the other side of Bridge Road. Ray Lodge was taken over by Riversdale Grenfell when the Pococks left, and then in 1865 by William Lassell, a well known astronomer of whom his friend Sir John Herschel said 'he belongs to that class of observer who created their own instrumental means'.

William Lassell was born in 1799 and had already mapped out a brilliant career before coming to Maidenhead. In 1820 and 1844 he had constructed his own reflecting telescopes, the latest of which he took to Malta in 1852 and discovered the satellites of several planets. When he took up residence at Ray Lodge he built an observatory in the garden which comprised a circular building on a square base with a flat roof through which a telescope protruded. At Maidenhead he set up a 2ft reflector and observed a black transit of Jupiter's satellite in December 1871. He died in October 1880 and had the distinction of being the first to be buried in St Luke's Churchyard under the new Burials Act.

The Ray Lodge Estate began to break up around 1910 and by 1932 the house had been turned into flats. Ray Drive was built within the estate and then in 1927 six pairs of semis were erected by the Empire Building and Trading Company which by 1930 had become known as Lassell Gardens after the astronomer. The base of the wall

Ray Lodge

133

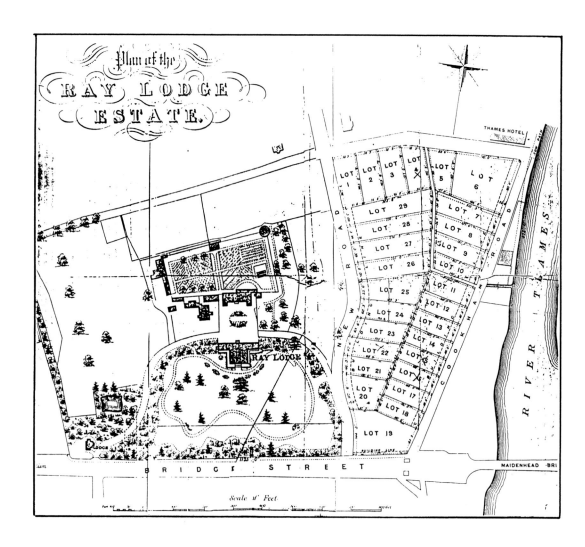

which once encircled the estate can be seen by the footpath in Bridge Road, while a stone outside Barclays Bank on the parade marks the position of the gatehouse.

Today the Ray family, who made their fortunes from bread and water, have long gone but their name lives on by the riverside. The island, on which they once ground their flour, is now a public park, giving pleasure to artists, tourists and residents alike.

Maidenhead road bridge represents the border between the ancient hundreds of Cookham and Bray, and it was the building of this structure that put Maidenhead on the map and eventually lessened the importance of the settlement of Cookham. Before the bridge Maidenhead had existed as the sleepy village of South Aylington and was subordinate to the two ancient manors.

The first wooden bridge was built in the thirteenth century, and most historians give a date of 1280 for its erection. However as early as 1255 Henry III issued an order for 'widening the road between Maidenhead Bridge and Henley' which would infer that it was in existence at this time. The bridge was made of wood for some 500 years before it was replaced by the present stone structure. It was longer than its successor and was situated north of its present position.

Due to heavy traffic the bridge was forever in a state of disrepair, and when Leland passed through the town in 1538 he commented that *'there is a great wharfage of timber and firewood on the west end of the bridge, and this wood cometh from Berkshire and the great woods and forest of Windsor and the Thicket.'* The wood he mentioned was obviously for bridge repairs. For the repair of the structure maintenance grants of pontage, or tolls, were repeatedly made to the sovereign, the earliest recorded being in 1297.

The bridge suffered during the many wars when again and again it was broken down. The most vivid wartime event took place in 1400 when a group of conspirators, supporters of Richard II, made an abortive attempt on the life of Henry IV. They retreated by way of Colnbrook to Maidenhead where they held the bridge for three days. During this time not one man passed over the river, and they captured from Henry two packhorses, two wagons and a chariot.

It was the custom in the Middle Ages for hermitages to be established on most bridges, and Maidenhead had such a structure which is described as adjoining the bridge on the west side and as having been rebuilt in 1423. The hermits were appointed by the diocese, and while dwelling in the hermitage accepted gifts from passers-by. After taking enough to pay for their bare necessities, they handed over the surplus which went towards the upkeep of the bridge. In the year 1423, presumably after the hermitage had been rebuilt, the Salisbury Registers gave an account of the induction of Richard Ludlow as the Maidenhead hermit.

From the time of its erection the wooden bridge was repaired numerous times to accommodate additional traffic. By a charter of James I the town acquired the right to take three oak trees annually from the royal manors of Cookham and Bray, and by 1735 this had been increased to twenty oaks. The bridge was repaired for the last time in 1750 at a cost of £764. Twenty years later it was deteriorating again and the Corporation applied to Parliament for permission to build a new structure. This was granted in 1772, and the Corporation accepted the plans submitted by Robert Taylor for the creation of a stone bridge. This was built by John Townsend of Oxford and was opened to the public in 1777.

From the outset tolls were collected on the new bridge and the toll gates stood near the Thames Riviera Hotel. Eventually the tolls were abolished in 1903 and the gates ceremoniously thrown into the river.

Lond.Mag. April 1780.

Maidenhead Bridge c. 1780

*The Royal Hundred
of Cookham*

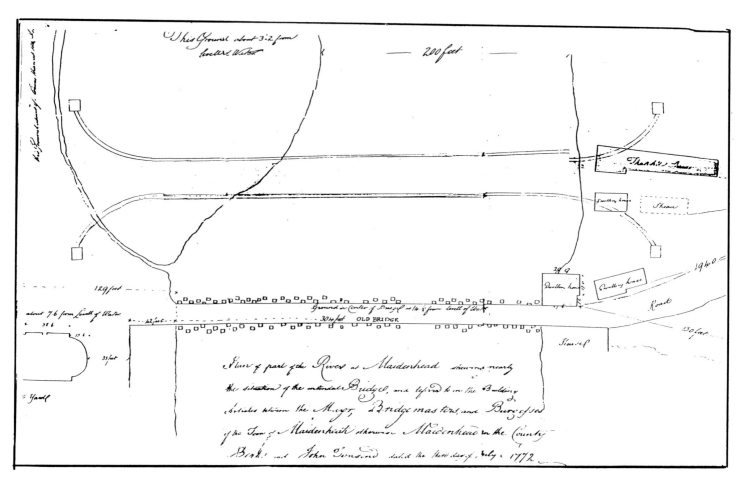

A Plan drawn in 1772 showing the position of the present bridge in relation to the old wooden structure

138

APPENDIX

Mention has been made of the two existing Anglo-Saxon documents which give evidence of the early monastery and possible royal meeting place at Cookham. Below is a literal translation of the documents giving full details of these occurrences:

An agreement between Archibishop Aethelheard and Abbess Cynethryth concerning the ownership of the monastery at Cookham dated A.D. 798

Æthelheard, by the grant of the abundant grace of Almighty God metropolitan of the church of Canterbury, with our most excellent King Cenwulf, summoning together all our provincial bishops, ealdormen and abbots and men of whatever high rank, to a synodal council in the place which is called *Clofesho*, there asked of them by careful inquiry how the catholic faith was held among them, and how the Christian religion was practised. To these inquiries it was unanimously replied thus: "Be it known to thy Paternity that exactly as it was set down in the beginning by the holy Roman and apostolic see, by the direction of the most blessed Pope Gregory, thus we believe, and we endeavour as much as we can to practise what we believe without equivocation." But after these things had been dealt with more fully, I began thus: "It is necessary, dearest brothers, to make restitution to the churches of God and the venerable men who for a long time now have been miserably afflicted by the loss of lands and the removal of title-deeds."

After these words, the documents of the monastery which is called Cookham, and of the lands adjacent to it, were produced in the midst. This monastery, namely with all the lands belonging to it, Æthelbald, the famous king of the Mercians, gave to the church of the Saviour which is situated in Canterbury, and in order that his donation might be the more enduring, he sent a sod from the same land and all the deeds of the afore-mentioned monastery by the venerable man Archbishop Cuthbert, and ordered them to be laid upon the altar of the Saviour for his everlasting salvation. But after the death of the aforesaid pontiff, Dægheah and Osbert, whom the same pontiff had brought up as pupils, impelled by the evil spirit, stole these same documents, and delivered them to Cynewulf, king of the West Saxons. And he, receiving immediately the evidence of documents, took over for his own uses the aforesaid monastery with all things duly belonging to it, disregarding the words and actions of the aforenamed Archibishop Cuthbert. Again, archbishops Bregowine and Jænberht complained through their various synods concerning the injury sustained by the church of the Saviour, both to Cynewulf, king of the West Saxons, and to Offa, king of the Mercians, who seized from King Cynewulf the oft-mentioned monastery, Cookham, and many other towns, and brought them under Mercian rule.

At length, King Cynewulf, led by a tardy penitence, sent back to the church of Christ in Canterbury the charters, that is to say, the deeds which he had wrongfully received from the above-mentioned men Dægheah and Osbert, with a great sum of money, humbly asking that he might not be imperilled under an anathema of so great authority. Truly, King Offa as long as he lived retained the afore-mentioned monastery, Cookham, without documents, just as he had received it, and left it to his heirs after him without the evidence of documents.

But in the second year of King Cenwulf, a synod was held at *Clofesho*, as has been indicated above. And I, Æthelheard, by the grace of God archbishop of Canterbury, and Cufa my dean with me, and many other seniors of that church of Christ, brought the deeds of the aforesaid monastery of Cookham into the council; and when they had been read through in the presence of the synod, it was decided by the voice of all that it was right that the metropolitan church should receive the oft-mentioned monastery, Cookham, whose title-deeds it had in its possession; because it had been so wrongly despoiled for such a long time.

Then, however, it pleased me, Æthelheard, by the grace of God archbishop, and Abbess Cynethryth, who at the time was in charge of the oft-mentioned monastery, and the elders assembled for this purpose from both sides, Kent, namely and *Bedeford*, that the same Cynethryth should give to me in exchange for the oft-mentioned monastery land of 110 hides in the region of Kent: 60 hides, namely in the place which is called Fleet, and 30 in the place which is called Tenham, and 20 in a third place which is called the source of the Cray. These lands, truly, King Offa formerly caused to be assigned to himself while he was alive and to his heirs after him, and after the course of their life, he ordered them to be consigned to the church which is situated at *Bedeford*. This also we decided in the presence of the whole synod that the abbess should receive from me the oft-mentioned monastery with its documents, and I should receive from her the lands and the deeds of the lands in Kent which she gave to me, to the end that no controversy may arise in the future between us and our heirs and those of King Offa, but that what was confirmed between us with the testimony of so noble a synod may be kept for ever by an unbroken covenant. I, Archbishop Æthelheard, also concede to the possession of Abbess Cynethryth the monastery which is situated in the place which is called *Pectanege*, which the good King Ecgfrith gave and granted by charter for me to possess with hereditary right.

The Witan, or government, meet at Cookham under King Aethelred the Unready A.D. 996–7

Here is made known, in this writing, how king Æthelred has granted that Ætheric of Bocking's testament might stand. It was many years before Ætheric deceased, that it was said to the king that he was of that evil counsel, that Sweyn should be received in Essex, when he first came thither with a fleet. And the king, before a great number of witnesses, made it known to archbishop Sigeric, who was then his advocate, on account of the land at Bocking, which he had bequeathed to Christchurch. Then was he, for this charge, both during life and after, unabsolved and without having made atonement, until his relict brought his heriot to the king at Cookham, where he had assembled his 'witan' from afar. Then would the king, before all his 'witan', prefer the charge, and said that Leofsige aldorman and many men were cognisant of the charge. Then the widow prayed archbishop Ælfric, who was her advocate, and Æthelmær, that they would pray the king that she might give her morning-gift to Christchurch, for the king and all his people, provided the king would abandon the terrible accusation, and that his testament might stand; that is, as it is here before said, the land at Bocking to Christchurch, and his other landed property to other holy places, as his testament declares. Then, may God requite the king, he consented to this, for love of Christ, and St Mary, and St Dunstan, and all the saints who rest at Christchurch, on the condition that she perform this, and his testament should stand fast. This declaration was straightways written, and read before the king and the 'witan'. These are the names of the men who of this were witnesses:

Ælfric archbishop, and Ælfeh, bishop of Winchester, and Wulfsige bishop of Dorchester, and Godwine bishop of Rochester, and Leofwine ealdorman, and Ælfsige abbot, and Wulfgar abbot, and Byrhtelm abbot, and Lyfincg abbot, and Ælfwold abbot, and Æthelmær, and Ordulf, and Wulfget, and Fræna, and Wulfric Wulfrun's son, and all the thanes who were there gathered from afar, as well of West Saxons as of Mercians, as of Danes and of Angles. Of this writing there are three: one is at Christchurch, the second in the king's treasury, the third the widow has.

Index to Selected People and Places